PRISONER OF HIS OWN THOUGHTS

THE STUDENT ATHLETE STORY

MICHAL GORSZCZARYK

D1521607

To all athletes who want to face the challenge of succeeding in their sports careers.

Recognize your small achievements, but always follow your bigger dreams.

To my family and mentors.

Thank you that you have always been there for me. You are the ones who taught me how to look at the bigger picture. If I could wish somebody only one thing — I would wish them to have people like you.

CONTENTS

INTRODUCTION   9

Part One
THE BEGINNING OF MY FIRST PATH

1. IT ALL BEGINS   15
2. LEAVE IT BEHIND   17
3. LEARNING FROM THE   21
   BETTER ONES
4. MENTORING PART 1   27
5. WALK IN   33
6. HIGH SCHOOL — THE FIRST YEAR   39
7. THE SECOND YEAR   49
8. THE LAST YEAR   61
9. MENTORING PART 2   81
10. RUSHING BACK   95
11. THE REALITY   99
12. HOBBIES   103
13. BIG SURPRISE   113
14. THE FIRST SEASON   127
15. THE SYSTEM   145
16. THE SECOND SEASON   153
17. THE CAPTAIN — THE LEADER   169
18. WHAT HAPPENS NEXT?   179
    TO BE CONTINUED   191

Part Two
THE PASSION = THE FUTURE

19. THE END...   195
20. ...THE BEGINNING   199
21. THE RISK   203
22. THE USA MODULE   209

23. MENTORING BEGINS   213
24. OTHER OPPORTUNITIES   217
25. MY FUTURE GOALS   221

Epilogue   225

About the Author   227

INTRODUCTION

DO I REALLY WANT THIS? — My favorite question.

People might not believe me, but I sit down to write this book. I already tried to compose before, but I could not finish this journey. I love to hear questions about what I want to do in my life, and the answers should be simple, incredibly simple. However, they are more problematic than you think. Do you really want this? If yes, just keep doing your thing. This one question can make you fall apart and hate the world around, or prove that you are in the correct place, but is it worth it? To be honest with you, for now I can tell you one factor. With the time, the answers change prior to the unique life situations and places where you are at. The beauty of it is that you always have to come back to that one question… Do you really want this? If yes, just keep working, but what if you don't want to? Are you going to give up? Trust me, finding the answer is not that simple.

Emotions are very important, yet can they let you down? I've learned that sometimes life will not go your way. You can put your head down and explain to yourself, "I did my best, maybe this is not for me". However, then again, like everyone reads your mind, this one question comes up – "Do I really want this?". If yes, don't quit right now. You cannot do that to yourself. Even though you wouldn't enjoy this as much as before, you have something that others don't, yet you don't know it. Moreover, imagine that you worked for something your entire life, and you never saw the opportunity coming for you. This moment might not come. And all signs would tell you, you shouldn't continue this path. It makes little sense now. Emotions would let me down, but the positive character will tell me to give it one more shot, to try again. Just one last time.

If I had quit before, I wouldn't have been writing this for you. I am the one who has been kicked all the time by life, and all signs has told me that soccer was not for me. I worked hard enough to achieve some success, but I cannot be the greatest. Some people let me down before, even my head coach. Later my own emotions, I couldn't handle the pressure. Then I was kicked again, and I got injured. I was never supposed to come back on the field, but I did. You would think the story ended, but not that fast. I came back to the sport after facing many challenges — finally, with significant opportunities to develop, and here we are again. Now, most likely, the NCAA system will not allow me to play anymore. I think you already know my favorite question. Do I really want this? The answer is — I don't know, what are the conditions? Luckily for me, being a player is not the only one solution. I love coaching, but quitting something what I love is the toughest part of my life. I just don't want to give up the chance of being great. Welcome to my story.

THE BEGINNING OF MY FIRST PATH

PRISONER OF HIS OWN THOUGHTS

PLAYER'S EYES

ONE

IT ALL BEGINS

I always like to hear the story of the beginning. That's why I will tell you mine. My family relationship has developed into a crazy one from the early stage. Since I remember, my mom wasn't with my dad. Most people would complain like I did. On the other side, I liked that time since I got many gifts from my parents. One day, my father came to Poland and took me for our first trip to the Czech Republic. I recall only two things from that trip. First, I got my first soccer practice kit. My dad brought me jersey of his favorite team — Chelsea. I received a small size of Lampard's gear, with number 8 on the back. Second, the trip ended much earlier than it was supposed to because I ate too much pierogi ruskie — my favorite dish — and got sick. Even though the trip wasn't the best for my old man, I enjoyed it. Furthermore, that was the beginning of something special for me. First actual contact with the ball. First favorite player. First dreams about soccer. After I took my jersey, my nickname was Lampard for my entire childhood. As you could guess, Chelsea has turned into my favorite club.

The beauty of being a kid is that your voice and your ideas don't matter for adults. Even when your own parents ask you "Who do you want to be when you grow up?", most likely they care little. Only with the years, your answer becomes more important for them. With that being said, one day me and my mom, Asia, went skiing. Even now, she still reminds me of that day. That time I told her for the first time about my soccer plans and said, "I will play in Chelsea, and I will be the best player over there". I wish to find those people who were sitting next to us on the ski lift, they had a lot of fun when they heard it... My mom laughed so much as well. Like I mentioned before, when you are young, your intentions aren't real for older people because they think that they know how the life goes.

TWO

LEAVE IT BEHIND

I was growing up in the minor city, Zgorzelec. I had plenty of friends and was spending a lot of time outside right after my classes. Playing around, having fun, looking for troubles — that's how I grew up. My mom always had to remind about the lunch from the balcony; otherwise, I wouldn't eat for the entire day. Time was running so quickly, I really enjoyed that. In addition, my friends and I were playing at the same team — Nysa Zgorzelec. Most of us had the same dream — to play soccer at the top level one day. Nobody knew how much we needed to invest and sacrifice to achieve that goal. In other words, we were just kids who had fun of playing soccer.

Despite all the fun I had, my family was worrying about me because I wasn't a brilliant student in the school. I was this naughty kid who didn't see the reasons to study at all. When I am looking back at that moment of my life, I understand that I got some help to move forward and find the better approach. At some point, my friends were choosing the different action — they stopped playing soccer for real. I was different; I didn't need to stop, and for sure I didn't want to go their way; I didn't want to smoke, drink, and catch other unwelcome habits. So, for the first time, I had to make my own decision, "I will still play". Slowly, I recognized that because I lived in the small city, it would be harder for me to reach bigger goals in soccer. If I wanted to play, I had to look for some changes.

I was failing in all potential ways; I was bad at home, terrible in school, and, as a teenager, I was cursing a lot. In other words, I lost my family's trust. Each argument with my mom ended badly because I constantly had something to resist. However, it was different with my grandfather, much different. If I tried to counter his speeches, I would really regret that. My grandpa is the only one who is tough for me, and I am difficult for him as well. He likes to talk so much; he is like a mentor because of his experience. Without playing around, my grandfather, Leszek, always tells me what he thinks. I am so glad that Dorota, my grandmother, can calm everyone down, so I can regularly get something from our talks. Otherwise, all of us would be just pissed off.

I loved to play video games, yet one day my grandfather walked into my room and made another mentor speech. He asked me if I preferred to be the best in the video games or on the field. That was enough to kick my butt off the chair. By the way, I have got the talent for making lengthy speeches after him. Sorry to all my friends because they all have to listen to my mentor talks.

That is how the tremendous change in my life started. I wished to prove that I could truly play soccer. To begin with this transformation, I studied more, practiced more, and was the best version of myself. For the first time, I put everything on the table. It was actually hard for me from the beginning — many times I had to say no to my friends, and some of them didn't like it. Today we are not close anymore. Some people might tell you that tremendous changes don't happen over the night, but trust me, enormous things can happen after only one talk. You just have to see the full image of things you undoubtedly want. I bet that my grandfather doesn't remember that day and his talk because he has made a lot of speeches during his life. Luckily for me, I remember that one.

I always thought people didn't pay attention for what I was doing, but I couldn't be more wrong. As soon as I did my homework on time, my grades immediately went up. Not only I got A's but also people noticed that I was trying to become a better student. After some time, I was well-organized, and school became very easy for me.

From the student who caused many problems in school, I became the guy who could make his mom proud. She was receiving only positive feedback about me. Those days, I was practicing a lot — minimum two times per day on the soccer field. Like my grandfather has told me, I was working to break my own limits. I pushed myself to the sky and guess what — everyone treated me with some respect. First time I could say that I carried everything right, and that's the reason why I could count on everyone's help with my next steps.

One day, I came to my mom to ask for help. I told her I wanted to play at the better level, so I might've had to leave to another city to continue my success. Of course, she helped me immediately. My mom knew that I was ready, all my family realized that. This one change helped me a lot, and it was simply about doing my duties right — I had to follow all directions, that's it. As the book goes, you will see how many benefits I picked up only because of my attitude, and not because I am the magnificent soccer player — I am not yet. Me and my mom looked for some options, and the best place was Wroclaw. It scared everyone to send me alone to the big city. Not because I would get lost, they knew that I would be fine. The reasons were clear, I was just fifteen years old; however, we all were happy about my decision, and I was so excited about my new challenge.

THREE

LEARNING FROM THE BETTER ONES

B eing from the minor city has some advantages, such as everyone knows each other, everything is close, the downtown might offer many activities without overcrowding it, but overall, I was not the happiest based on my own possibilities in that town. The soccer industry was visibly very poor. I didn't have the best quality facilities to develop, and to be more specific, I didn't have a true goalkeeper coach until I was fifteen years old. My first regular goalkeeper practice was offered by my high school, SMS Junior Wroclaw. Before that, I won the goalkeeper position in Zgorzelec; however, I wasn't challenged enough for the starting spot. Many people might think stability is essential, but for me it's not challengeable. Staying in the comfort zone would never push me through the tremendous soccer industry.

As a young athlete who was looking for some changes, I couldn't wait for support anymore. I didn't even know anybody who could help me with moving forward. The strongest alternative to start was to write an email and hope that somebody would find a minute to open and read it thoroughly. That was my only shot.

It is hard to say what messages work for coaches. For sure, the references can be the most relevant, but let's focus on dealing with it with no contacts. If you can detect a coach on social media, I would use each way to contact them. That is your responsibility to find an excellent team. Coach just wouldn't mind putting another skillful player in the roster. That's why this industry is brutal. When you are at the top level, you always have to compete with other brilliant players. Only the best of the best can earn this spot. Are you ready for it?

I was definitely looking for that challenge. My family was with me, and I had all support from their side. I was sending a lot of emails and reaching out to the teams on my own. However, I had to resend them many times before getting some answers. To be honest with you, big clubs will not answer you until you bother them a lot. You have to be very lucky that your email is first on the screen when coach logs into their email. You need to have some tools, like good highlights, good resume, etc. That's how soccer looks nowadays. I didn't have any of those, I would never think I needed to record myself on practices and games because, as a kid, I didn't care much about doing any research — I just sent a lot of emails with my personal information. I found the message, which I texted to the coach from Śląsk Wroclaw on his Facebook account. You can laugh at it as much as you want:

"I am a goalkeeper. I was born in 30th December 1996. I am training and playing in my home team, MKS Nysa Zgorzelec, and I would like to try myself in Śląsk Wroclaw. Are there any chances to do it? When can I come for practice?"

After years, I am still laughing at it. Please, ask your parents to help you out with the message before you will send something to important people. As an unknown player, the first step in order to get an answer from any coach you haven't met yet is to make a wonderful impression.

Even though getting some answers from coaches was hard, they invited me for a practice to Śląsk Wroclaw. I reached out to the goalkeeper coach who said that I could come any Monday at 4 pm. With that being said, me and my mom didn't wait long, and on the upcoming Monday we were ready for the big trip. Finally, it was the first big chance for me to shine. Like I mentioned before, I have never had a regular goalkeeper practice in my life before going to the tryouts in Śląsk. It was a tremendous event for me because it was the first time when I saw a well-organized practice. I accomplished one of my funda-mental goals — I got my chance to show my skills, which weren't great at all. Therefore, I would never know that if I wouldn't send the emails.

I came for my first professional GK practice. Like always, I arrived before everything started, so I could have some time for myself. I looked around at those nice facilities. Since I arrived to Śląsk, I knew that I wanted to play for them. The whole practice wasn't hard at all, it was the basic stuff. However, I didn't have the basic tools and I have never been coached that way. Other goalkeepers were professionals for me that day. They were flying in the air while the guy from the minor city hit the ground with each dive. From one drill to another, I was getting proofs that I was far behind — there was a vast gap between us already at that age. Normally, I would be sad and happy at the same time. This situation would have told me it's time to let it go, it's enough for me, and it's time to stop playing soccer. Time for the plan B in my life. But years ago, I was much different; I was a kid who just got kicked to work harder. The goal-keeper coach told me I wasn't ready to play in Śląsk Wroclaw yet because I didn't have enough basic skills. However, he told me I should try next time. I should practice first, get another experience in games, and then come back again. I never came back on my own without a special invitation to Śląsk Wroclaw.

This was one of the most important experiences in my young career. Without it, I would still believe that I could reach the sky with my soccer skills. I was super wrong about my ego, but that was a life lesson for me. To find a genuine challenge, face better players. To be a top quality player, you must convince an unknown person from the stands to write your name down on the scouting list. Otherwise, you always think you are an outstanding athlete, and at the end of the day, the story will end with no results.

Do you still remember the message which I sent to the coach on Facebook? The coach, Ryszard Pietraszewski, never answered me for that message, I sent it on September 24th, 2011. Guess what happened later... I worked with this coach for 4 years. Coach Pietraszewski recommended me to one of the best academies in Poland. In addition, he convinced the coaching staff to invite me for the official tryouts. As I said before, I never came back just for another practice; instead, I entered to get my enormous deal done. After my high school years, he was the one who got me into semi-pro level where he was the head coach at that time. When I told him that he didn't reply to me a few years ago, we both laughed. Yeah, this is a hilarious story. Thank you, coach, for everything because without you I wouldn't be able to make it this far.

FOUR

MENTORING PART 1

GK CAMP "PIERWSZY BRAMKARZ" ("FIRST GOALKEEPER")

I would never force myself to work hard for the long time without getting any extra motivation. Even the best computer software needs new updates. I just can't do my job without seeing a progress and facing fresh challenges. Believe me or not, but most people have the same thing, they are quitting because they cannot find the recent update for their own software. As I already mentioned, I was looking for this challenge. I went for practice to Śląsk Wroclaw, but I wasn't good enough back then. If I had to illustrate my soccer dream, it would be something very close to what I saw in Śląsk. That's why I was mad — I wanted to be at that stage a few years ago. This madness pushed me forward a lot of times, but I had to find something new, something better because an update was necessary.

Summer was nearby, that year I didn't think about anything else than soccer. I wanted to get into the best goalkeeper camp in Poland. My parents made some research, and somehow, I ended up going to Gutów Mały. My mom dropped me at the first goalkeeper camp in my life. I met the coaches and operation staff, received my keys, and went to the room to organize my things. That was a very long way to drive, but thank you, mom, for taking me over there. I was so excited to start my first professional trainings.

I went with no friends to that camp — I didn't know anybody. However, with no problems, I met other goalkeepers. When all people have the same hobby, it is very easy to make friends. Almost every camper my age or a bit younger was already a big time player. People could find national team appearances and very popular soccer academies in their resumes. I was impressed, but at the same time very jealous because I was never close enough to enjoy soccer that much yet. For them it was like a normal summer, just the next goalkeeper camp. I didn't know what to expect at all. For me it was something exceptional.

During the camp goalkeepers were separated into small groups, so everyone could get as many repetitions as possible. The level was on the top; I remember that even my roommate, Kamil, the player from GKS Bełchatów, was about to sign the contract with

Feyenoord Rotterdam — that was big for me. After a few years, one goalkeeper from the younger group signed with TSG 1899 Hoffenheim. Both of the teams are playing at the highest level in their countries. Feyenoord plays at first division in Netherlands and Hoffenheim in Germany. So, now you can imagine the level of the camp.

Furthermore, during the camp we could see the youth Poland national team. They had the camp at the same time; sometimes I could see some drills while we were walking to get a meal. I have never been offered to attend more professional camps. Each drill was important for me, I was trying to understand and repeat the smallest details to become a better goalkeeper. Sometimes I was trying too hard, and my emotions took control over me. I remember one drill — passing exercise, finding the player without the ball on the full speed. Coach Krzyształowicz got very mad at me since my passes were very soft, and I was moving very slow on the goal. He told me to get some rest if I didn't want to work on the full speed. I got very mad, but not at my coach, I was mad at myself. At the end of the drill, I asked if I could do it one extra time. Without being shy, I think I did the exercise on the better speed than everyone else. I showed that I was the best in that drill, and coach finally told me I did a wonderful job. That was one of the best feelings I have ever had during the practice. I bet that he doesn't even remember that, but after that drill, I knew that I would love to work with this coach regularly. He was tough, but he had exceptional experience and knowledge; that was what I needed. Coach Krzyształowicz has become my mentor, and that one drill was special for me.

In my mind, the mentor is somebody who has a tremendous impact on your daily life. They can help you become a better person just because of their presence. They might not even be aware of that. The mentor makes you work harder than ever. This person cannot be easy for you, even if the mentor is your best friend, there is time to work and time to joke; mentor knows how to manage it. If you think your world is falling apart, the mentor always says something that makes you to believe in your dreams again. The mentor always is there for you to help, they care about your success. This person doesn't charge you for an advice, the mentor is always there for you when you need it.

That week of work was something special for me, but it ended quickly. I didn't want to go back home to the normal life. I remember how my mom came to pick me up, and how I asked her to buy me goalkeeper gloves and to talk with coach about his thoughts about me. His opinion was very important for me. I was sitting outside, waiting for my mom. I couldn't wait to hear what coach would say about me, especially after seeing me with much better goalkeepers. I was nervous because my mom talked with the coach for so long, and I already came up with all scenarios. Finally, my mom came back, and I felt that she was happy after the talk. I was listening to all the details with the enormous smile on my face. Overall, coach said that I wasn't a good goalkeeper yet because I didn't have a lot of tools. However, he knew that I never had a goalkeeper coach who I could work regularly with. That's why he was very impressed of how I presented on the camp. He said that I had something special that put me in front of many goalkeepers. That message is in my head till today, and it still helps me to defeat many difficulties on my way. Coach said that he couldn't wait to see my progress after some time in SMS Junior Wroclaw (my high school).

Even though I have a few mentors in my life, coach Krzyształowicz is one of the biggest ones, and, with no doubt, he is the best goalkeeper coach I have ever worked with. In this book, you will meet all my mentors. Without them, I could never push beyond my limits and achieve any goals in my life. You can't predict when and where you will meet somebody important. This camp was one of the best camps I have ever gone to. Moreover, I have received much more than just goalkeeper skills; I met one of the most important coaches in my life. Mentoring is one of the most important details. Look for it! You might need someone's help with facing some difficulties in your life.

· · ·

LITTLE NOTE FOR COACH KRZYSZTAŁOWICZ:

"Hello coach, if you are reading this book please know that without you I would never believe in myself that I can play soccer at a professional level. Without your help, I would never fight for it. Without you, I wouldn't become the person who I am today. Thank you for being my mentor."

FIVE

WALK IN

S ome people get the biggest benefits while the others make the simplest mistakes. I remember the time when I was waiting for the information if there was a spot in a camp with my new club, Parasol Wroclaw. I didn't even know what I could expect; I didn't know anybody over there, but I wanted to move forward. I was bothering my mom to call their coach every day to check if he had some updates for me; however, I was scared to call on my own, and I actually never talked to that coach before. One day before the camp, his goalkeeper didn't show up for the day of physical exams. The coach, Janusz Siepietowski, was the old school coach, so he had very strict rules. That goalkeeper didn't want to follow it at all, so he was out of the camp which meant that he was out of the squad for that season. The spot opened for me one day before the departure to the camp. I couldn't waste that shot, let's go!

No matter where you are coming from, no matter what kind of person you are, it is always hard to walk into an unknown place. Some people like to face this pressure, others would rather avoid that. Even though I didn't like the pressure, I knew that there was no other way than walking in and introducing myself as a new goalkeeper. Most of the time, people have to prove to themselves that they are ready to make progress and change.

As soon as I arrived at my new team's facilities, I wanted to go back home immediately. How many times have you seen abandoned place? Furthermore, how many times in your life have you decided to work for that place? That was crazy for me. The building with all the locker rooms was about to fall any minute. The major field was in a very poor condition, and the eighteen yards box was horrible. Later in the season, I understood the difference between diving on the asphalt and diving on our field — the asphalt in the parking looked nicer. However, the last results were the same; my body was hurt literally every day.

As I mentioned before, I wanted to leave that place as soon as I saw it. However, my mom convinced me to give it a shot and talk with the coach. Otherwise, we would just waste his time, and I wouldn't have any place to play in the upcoming season. Coach Siepietowski didn't wait long to introduce me to the team, he immediately treated me as a part of his family. Maybe it wasn't one of the best walk-ins I have ever had, but it was the funniest one for sure. He kept me in the front of the entire team, asking me questions, and suddenly I had to introduce myself in English. Back then I didn't speak English at all.

"Hi, my name is Michal Gorszczaryk, I am from Zgorzelec." — That was all I could say.

That was a brilliant start before the camp.

His personality proved that the facilities weren't the most important thing back then. He had something unique, and I saw it from the beginning. He could convince the whole team to work hard. If you were the best player, he would make you become the leader of the squad. Moreover, that coach didn't have any favorites, and everyone was treated equally. The team was always for him, and he was always for the club. Trust me, that's very rare to find. It wasn't about becoming the best individual player, everything was about building the best team in the league.

Back then, Parasol Wroclaw just went to the lower division after their last season. With that being said, we didn't play at the highest level. However, all professionals know that one of the hardest things to achieve is to get promoted immediately after being placed at the lower division. Our team target was very simple — to make it happen. The full team was working hard during the entire camp. In the early morning we ran a lot — because our coach loved to run! He ran with us, can you believe it? After that, quick breakfast, and later we went back to sleep. Before noon we headed to the first practice on the field. Oh, trust me, it wasn't easy at all, soccer drills and conditioning exercises at the same time. That could break everyone — you don't believe me, do you? Let me set the meeting with coach Siepietowski. Later in the day, we had a lunch break, and then some time for us. We didn't have time to rest because before the dinner, we had another full session on the field. If we were doing the exercises correctly, we didn't have to do conditioning drills after the practice. But imagine — if your legs were soft, could you kick the ball on the money? Well, I met some players that could do it. We just ran a couple of times on the evening practice — it wasn't bad. In addition, I was so amazed at how that coach handled the whole team alone, including goalkeepers. He was everywhere; in addition, as time showed me, that coach was special.

At the end of every camp, there is always some routine for the new members. People who just joined the team had to complete some tasks which were made by athletes and coaching staff. This was one of the best times of the camp, but mostly only for the players and coaches who have done it before. During our camp, we had other new players, so I wasn't alone. I recall that everyone was hanging in the hotel room, and then two players came to pick me up. They covered my head, so I couldn't see where I was heading to. I saw nothing until we got to the special place. Everyone was there, waiting for the freshmen. After we arrived, coaching staff and players created some tasks that had to be completed. I remember that I had to dance with the soccer ball. It was fun, and the next day we got back to home. The whole squad became one unit. I had great feelings about the upcoming season.

In the meantime, high school was about to start; however, that time, the walk in was much different for me. A lot of athletes from my team were attending the same high school as me, so I had an enormous confidence at that moment. Even though I didn't know anyone from my class, I had many friends outside the classroom. That was the easiest walk in I have ever had.

SIX

HIGH SCHOOL – THE FIRST YEAR

One of the most important things for all athletes is to see their own progress and success. If they do not see it, there are minimum two results. First, athletes will give up their dreams since they do not look at where their work is going to. They are exhausted because they are working hard, but at the end of the day, there is no happiness. No matter who you are, the situation is troublesome; however, most athletes often forget about the difference between being a competitor in the team sport and in the individual sport. People often forget about understanding how to look at success in different kinds of sports — especially young athletes. They are interested only in trophies and individual prizes. Otherwise, the taste of sport is not going to be the same as it was one year ago before investing hundreds of hours of your own time. Second way, athletes will keep working on their dreams since they know the difference between seeing unique types of achievements — a small one at the beginning and the huge/ultimate victory at the end of the sport career. Most people would wonder how long this athlete will continue working on their dreams with the same or even better work attitude. The answer is very complicated. But I know one thing — the attitude might change without a taste of fame and progress, and the taste of doing something great might turn into tough times. As a young athlete, you have to understand what target is available to reach by you. This will be your major motivation to keep working on your huge and future happiness.

Back then, before the high school, I placed myself into the second poll. I didn't give up and wanted to move forward, to achieve something huge and to be seen by others. Regardless of my determination and my sacrifice, I was a ticking bomb. If I didn't achieve and taste some profits from what I was doing, I would literally explode inside. Hiding an anger in front of other people is sometimes necessary; however, you cannot hide it from yourself. When you explode, you will lose everything what you have been working on. With that being said, you are going to drop to the poll number one and give up everything. I have achieved nothing yet; this was supposed to be my big FIRST YEAR.

Adjusting to the adult's life is hard when you are fifteen. I didn't know how to cook, wash my clothes, manage my money, and wake up on my own before 6 am. It was tough, and not because of the amount of activities, but because I had to become responsible for myself with that number of duties. I knew my goals, and finally I could test my attitude. However, when I look back, I wasn't at the worst place. When you are surrounded by people with the same dreams, it is very easy to make friends. Most of the time, they will be with you all the time and will become your best friends. I didn't feel alone with reaching my dreams.

I quickly made lots of friends at my new home, Wroclaw. Many of them came from outside as I did, so we lived together in the dorms. However, some of them stayed at home, and every morning they took a train to come to the school. I am not a morning person, so when I saw my schedule for the first time, I was extremely disappointed. I didn't know how I could get through waking up before 6 am to get to the school or practice. To be honest with you, I don't know how I managed it at all throughout my high school years. The schedule was very busy because I not only had classes at my school, but I also had to practice with my classmates since we were a part of sport school program, and later, I had practices with my team (almost every day). Usually, I got home around 8 pm, sometimes even later. Finally, I had time to eat and chill because the next morning I had to get up before 6am again. Good night.

There was literally nothing in my soccer resume. I didn't win anything, and nobody ever heard of me. It was the time to change that. The team spirit was on another level, and the class atmosphere during the school practices was fantastic. I have never experienced something better than that. I had grand feelings about my progress, so I couldn't find a better place to keep working hard. I was so determinate to reach another level in my career, and after many years, I got all the tools I needed. I was hoping to find somebody who knew how to coach me.

What I loved the most was the high speed of my life — I didn't slow down even for a second. I saw a lot of beauty in that. Going to the school by tram number 31 or 32, then going by any tram to the Parasol Wroclaw field — every single day except Sundays. I wouldn't be able to make it happen without all those people around me. They did the same, so our team knew what we were playing for. All of us wanted to do something special that year. We were required to get back to the highest division at the youth level; moreover, we wanted to be undefeated in our current division.

Finally, we were winning a game by game, and I was an enormous part of that team. Every single weekend we were celebrating and getting closer to achieve our goal. Even though we played many games, I never knew who we were facing each time. When people asked me who we played that day, I answered that I didn't know. I wasn't focused on the rival; I was focused on getting another three-point win. During that season, we had two goalkeepers in the roster — it was me and my friend. Coach wanted to be fair, so if nobody missed the practice, we played exactly the same amount of minutes (45 minutes each). If one of us skipped the team practice, then that person would start the second half or even end without playing at all. Even though I had practices every day with my school before team practices, I almost never skipped team trainings. My head coach knew how busy I was since he was the sport director back then at my high school. He was the one who saw my sacrifice every day. I received many benefits with that, and first huge success was coming shortly.

We finished our fall season undefeated; we literally destroyed our division. We were on the whole another level, but we still had to finish our job and stay undefeated till the end. At the same time, I was becoming a much better goalkeeper because I was working many hours on my goalkeeper skills. My investments paid me back, and many people saw me as a serious worker with a great potential to become a solid goalkeeper soon.

One day was special for me. It was a normal day at school; I was sitting by my desk, listening to the lecture. Then, out of nowhere, the director interrupted our class which he never did before. I was more surprised when he called my name and instructed me to follow him. We came to his office, and he told me to close the door and sit down. I was obviously scared, but I couldn't remember if I did something bad. However, that day was the most amazing day in my life back then. All my years I have been working to hear his words. He informed me that he received many calls from Śląsk Wroclaw and said that they were extremely interested in getting me for the next season. WOW!

You probably bet that I ended in Śląsk Wroclaw... If I could go back in time, I would end in Śląsk for sure. However, I am not the guy who can make hard decisions immediately. I don't remember if I told those news to anyone, because back then I was holding everything mostly for myself — the biggest mistake. Maybe only my parents knew about those calls, or maybe my best friend, Patryk Biegański, my roommate. To be honest with you, I didn't know what to do.

I was extremely delighted that somebody rooted for me; however, I was happy with my current team. My team and I were winning every single weekend. When Sunday evenings came, and Patryk got to the dorms, he was repeatedly asking what the score of the game was. It was obvious that we won. Also, coach Siepietowski was always grading each player after the games. Probably it was his method of keeping us motivated.

Each Monday, everyone was waiting to hear their grades from the previous game. The greatest score was 10, but you had to do everything perfect to receive it. For me, one of the most remarkable games in the season was against Pogoń Oleśnica because then I could face my classmates. We were working together every day, so whoever won that game would be the king in the class. Our team defeated Pogoń Oleśnica twice in that season — 4-0 and 0-3, so I was the king. With each argument or joke, I could always say: "If you want to talk with me, dial on the phone +04 then later +07", because we won by 7 goals in total. However, most importantly, I wanted to get the strongest grade for the games. After playing against Pogoń Oleśnica, coach Siepietowski told me I would get the highest grade, 10, if I wouldn't make a slight mistake. Of course, only he saw it. In his eyes, I made a foul, but the referee whistled nothing. At the end of the day I got 9, but this was the best motivation for me to keep working hard and finally get 10 points. When the season ended, I finished with two 10 points and a lot of 9s and 8s. The most important result was the championship and being the champion with winning every single game in that season. Look at the results on your own.

Season 2012/2013
Matches played — 27

Goals scored — 159

Goal against (lost) — 20

A1 Junior LEVEL

HTTPS://WWW.LACZYNASPILKA.PL/DRUZYNA-SEZON/PARASOL-WROCLAW/41571.HTML

Sometimes I wish that we could play at the highest division because we had the team that could have won everything back then. Coach Siepietowski created something special, and there was this magic in our team — the spirit. As an ultimate result, our team became the champion with the scores placed above. This was the best season I have ever had. I didn't want to change anything. Even though I saw coaches from Śląsk Wroclaw on our games, I wasn't sure if this was the time for me to leave. They wanted me in their team with no official tryouts, so I basically had the deal on the table. Back then, I thought I shouldn't have changed anything because I was winning everything. When I was asking for the advice about my future, I heard too many things and I was lost in my own thoughts. I made my last decision and stayed in Parasol Wroclaw. I don't know what I had in my mind; it scared me to get out of my comfort zone, but that was my first gigantic mistake that cost me a lot. I knew that coach Siepietowski would not be my head coach for the next seasons, but I wasn't aware that all he built would be gone. Moreover, I didn't know that the wonderful head coach and talented team were the key to achieve everything. Without that, I was literally nothing.

LITTLE NOTE for coach Siepietowski and his team:

"Hello coach, I wanted to thank you again for everything you did during that season for us. Thank you for staying with me after practices to work on my goalkeeper skills. I would never forget our workouts on the sand. I hated it so badly because I was exhausted after working with you, but the results came quickly. You pushed me to be a better person and a better player, you created something magic, something that happens very rare in sport. Thank you for being a magnificent coach and my mentor during those years in high school. In addition, I wanted to thank everyone who took an enormous part of this success. Without all my teammates, I wouldn't have those dominant memories and experience of winning and being the best. Thank you for pushing each other to become winners and better players."

SEVEN

THE SECOND YEAR

I couldn't wait for the next season because it was supposed to be my next big year. Unfortunately, coach Siepietowski couldn't be our head coach for the next season. Back then, the head coaches in the club were in charge only of one age group, and that was the last year for coach Siepietowski with our group before the next players joined the team. Even though coach Siepietowski built one of the best teams in the club, he had to step back because the year of 1996 was coming with their own head coach, Robert Cichy. Me and my teammates from the older group couldn't do anything about that.

Our new team with the new head coach went to the summer camp. Couple of players from the last season were returning, but it was a completely fresh team. We were preparing to play at the highest level at that time in our age group, but I couldn't remember if we had set some goals for that season during the summer camp. After my last season in Parasol, I was used to the high standard based on the season's major goals. For example, winning the conference with the specific amount of points. However, that time the attitude wasn't at the same level. The team was also much different, everything was very soft, there was no energy and no spirit. My teammates from last year and I could feel it. When we had some free time, we were comparing the preseason from the last year to that one, and we all got to the same conclusion — we came to take part in a great summertime, not a summer camp.

The preseason is the only time when all athletes want to give up; it is the hardest time for everyone. You must push yourself and throw all your energy on each practice. This is the toughest part of the season, but the beauty of it is that everyone is competing with their own mindsets, and only after winning this fight with yourself, you can compete against the teammates and other opponents. This is the time for a head coach to shine. Some athletes have the best coaches, so the fight with their mindset is very easy because their mentors know how to manage that. As I mentioned before, it is truly rare to find some-body who knows how to motivate other people to work hard. Even harder to meet a coach who knows how to create the best and the safest environment for all players. During my initial year, I was lucky to have this kind of coach. He knew everything about creating a great working atmosphere and getting the best out of each player. The fundamental goal was to win everything, and in the meantime, this has become the motto of the family — that's how the best friendships were created. Time with coach Cichy was much different. He just didn't have the same tools and mindset as coach Siepietowski. However, the worst thing was that I was inside the environment where friendship had a tremendous part of the important decisions. I wasn't against friendship, but during the practices we were joking more than we were preparing for the game. In addition, I, as a goalkeeper, wasn't used for most of the session — I was just staying on the sideline. I didn't blame the coach for that, but that was the first feeling when I knew that I wasn't at the best environment. Building friends in the team was important; however, I wanted to be a part of team where the goal was clear — CHAMPIONSHIP.

The environment where friends are the primary value of the team will not bring you any success. Everyone will complain about hard work because nobody is used to do that. Everyone will laugh no matter how the game goes. Everyone will participate for fun, not for achieving something special. As I mentioned before, my friends from the previous year and I were different. However, we couldn't change anything, even though we were asking coach Siepietowski to come back and take our team. It never happened.

Even though we played on a better level, I felt that I learned nothing. Moreover, the team practices were a total disaster for me. The coach almost never used goalkeepers, so most of the time I was just standing on the side and waiting for the time to be involved. Back then, our team had 3 goalkeepers in the roster. Of course, they let themselves skip some practices, but when they came, they wanted to have fun rather than work. I was pissed and wanted to transfer to Śląsk Wroclaw as soon as possible. I was so mad at myself because I made one of the worst decisions in my life — I didn't change the team when I was supposed to do it.

When people feel the waves, they should always follow them and never leave the water. With that being said, always look for better opportunities for yourself. If you get a better chance to shine, go for it without wondering what this wave will bring you. The most important thing is to get to the new wave. Remember my words.

First time in my life I hated to go to Parasol Wroclaw facilities. Everything because of the new team, new coaching staff, and new rules. It wasn't my world, and the season wasn't going well for us either. Even though we were winning some games, most of the time we played very poor. However, how I already mentioned, nobody cared about it except me and my few friends from the last season.

We were facing much better teams; for example, Śląsk Wroclaw. Even though the game was always close and tough, we were far away from them based on their soccer skills — they were just much better. Actually, a lot of teams were better than us, so our record was worse than last season. When you are winning everything, everyone will be interested in you. As soon as you lose your first game, trust me, your phone is going to be quiet unless your mom or friends are trying to reach out to you.

I was lucky that I was still a part of my high school, SMS junior Wroclaw. The atmosphere which we had there was keeping me to play soccer. I enjoyed every practice, especially the goalkeeper ones. Sometimes I hope that our school would have different politics, and rather than being just classmates, we could call each other teammates. Back then, the school only offered the prime quality coaches, facilities, and trainings, but not a team competition. Everyone was extremely engaged in playing soccer. When you are in the locker room with this kind of people, you cannot play bad, it's just not happening. Everyone works hard for each other — that's the soccer family. The reality was brutal, and it was not possible to find that kind of spirit in Parasol. To summarize, I loved my first part of the day — school time, but I hated the afternoon practices with my team. That is why I wanted to leave at all costs.

Unfortunately, my desire to leave wasn't enough for other teams. Our season wasn't that good like it was the last year, and as soon as they compared me to much more people, I wasn't that special anymore. To be more specific, I didn't have the same statistic as last year, but they didn't know that it was because of the team situation back then. The coaching staff changed, and it stole everything from me. That was the first time when I hated being on the practice. I didn't enjoy soccer; moreover, coaches could notice that. I was lucky that my mindset was much different in SMS (my high school), and because of that some people were trying to help me out. For example, my coach Ryszard Pietraszewski, from SMS, told me he would do his best to send me to Śląsk Wroclaw. Remember that coach who didn't answer me about tryouts? Now he was helping me on his own to get me over there. That's funny. I just had to keep working, so I did it. When I saw the light in the long tunnel, it motivated me enough.

The entire season was tough for me, and I was about to explode. I was a ticking bomb, and I would be gone soon without more lights in the tunnel. I was praying to get another chance to play for somebody who cared about their players, excellent results and progress at the same time. I just hoped to have a coach who would do his best to make my dreams come true. I was at the correct time with my skills and attitude, but not at the correct place.

Before I decided to stay in Parasol Wroclaw for the next season, I had one huge incident with my future coach. I remember the day when my friend told me he was invited for official tryouts to Śląsk Wroclaw. I was happy for him, but at the same time, I was jealous. Anyway, my friends and I decided to watch those tryouts. As soon as we got there, we saw our coach from the school who called me immediately. Coach Pietraszewski was standing with a goalkeeper coach from Śląsk, Waldek Grzanka, and they were very surprised that I wasn't changed and ready to play. Coaches asked me what happened, and why I wasn't on the field. I didn't know what to say because I knew nothing about my invitation to those tryouts. They told me they called to Parasol Wroclaw and talked with coach Cichy (not my head coach at that time) who was supposed to tell me all the information. Of course, he had plenty of time to tell me about my invitation, but he obviously didn't want to do it. On the next day, I came to his office and asked why he didn't inform me about my huge chance. All what he told me was that he just forgot about it. I was so pissed at him, but I let it go — I didn't want to make a big scene out of that. I didn't even tell my head coach about that incident, because he would just tell me to leave that place for the next season. I thought coach Cichy maybe really forgot about that, and at the end of the day, I was the one who didn't accept the offer to go to Śląsk. I couldn't be more wrong about declining the offer from them...

Coach Cichy just didn't care much about me, we didn't have the best relationship. I believe that he needed different players than me, and I couldn't count on his help. After some time, coach Pietraszewski convinced Śląsk to invite me for tryouts and give me another shot. I wanted to play for a better team with some soccer perspectives. One day, I got a call from goalkeeper coach, Grzanka, who invited me for a scrimmage against Legia Warsaw. I never played the game with that range of an opponent. I was super excited, but nervous at the same time. If everything went well, I would play for one of the best academies in Poland. I didn't tell those news even to my best friends, I just didn't want to feel more pressure. So, I just came to Śląsk Wroclaw's locker room where coaches and I talked about the game, and after that talk, I was supposed to be ready to play against Legia Warsaw.

In my mind, the game went well for me. I was proud that I dealt with that talented team. We tied that game, but we had much more chances to win it though. Our players just missed the opportunities. I made a couple of good saves; however, as the goalkeeper coach told me after the game, I made two vast mistakes which showed that I couldn't be a real goalkeeper. Oh, that was a tremendous hit for me. I knew that I made one mistake which caused us losing one goal; however, I wasn't the only one who messed up with that play. In addition, the second mistake the coach thought about wasn't even mine. However, his goalkeeper's vision was different, and I was the one who wanted to transfer. I had to play with his rules, and I couldn't satisfy his needs. At the end of the game, I left with nothing. Moreover, I lost even more; I lost my hopes that I would ever make it. I was happy that my family finally had time to watch my game, but I hoped they would end with celebrating my success rather than comforting me.

I didn't have pleasant mood at all; however, I knew that I needed to move forward with that. I talked with my mentor, coach Krzyształowicz, who told me to not take that opinion to my heart. He told me to keep my head up and believe in myself. Those little words set my head to work hard, only to prove coach Grzanka that he made a huge mistake. I was very pissed at him. However, right now I understand how the competition at the highest level works. I know that coaches have to make hard decisions with getting new players, and if I want to be one of them, I have to be better than all their current players and all their choices for that spot. I have to be the best of the best. Then this spot is for me.

I was mad at myself because I couldn't forget my vast mistake when I decided to stay in Parasol Wroclaw. I believe that I had the attitude to be the best, but all I needed was to be in the best system, and Śląsk Wroclaw offered that because their first team was playing at the highest level in Poland. Getting to the system where all you need to do is to make the next team in the club (from youth level to the senior level) is way easier than to compete for that one open spot at any level with all other players around the country. Especially when only one game will decide about your future. It might not be fair, but that's the brutal reality.

Back to my decision of declining the Śląsk's offer; I just wasn't aware of the consequences — the chances of playing big soccer were almost all gone for me. From the season which brought me to the sky and helped me with my dreams, I got to the spot where I started to hate soccer. That was the first time when I was mad at the ball, at myself, and everything around it. Please believe me, when you are in this kind of mood, don't expect that you will have a great season. It's not going to happen. If you are in this mood, try to run away to another place immediately...

Even though the season was bad for me, and my depressive mood reached all my limits, somehow, I got another chance to move forward. I was invited to tryouts to Miedź Legnica, another big time club which had the first team in the second highest division in Poland. When I first arrived to the dorms, I didn't like the place. It looked weird and very similar to the place I did my best to escape from. So, the first impression of my potential place didn't work for me at all. Of course, I wanted to try. The practices were excellent, and I really experienced the professionalism of that team. However, the president of the school didn't want to agree at my requests. I wanted to finish my school in Wroclaw and keep the same professors for the last year before mature exams. I wouldn't be able to trust some random teachers from another sports school with their methods of exam preparation. The deal was simple — I had to change my high school, and I had to do everything in Miedź Legnica. Even though I was suffering in Parasol Wroclaw, I couldn't leave something what I enjoyed the most, something what was keeping me with playing soccer, I couldn't leave SMS where I had the best time ever. I know that many people will not understand that, but I didn't have the best feelings in Miedź Legnica. I wasn't ready to say that I would love to sign the contract with them.

After the poor season and tough time, I hoped that coach Krzyształowicz would run some camp over the summer. However, I heard nothing about it, so I decided to reach out to the coach. Of course, my mom helped me with that. I got the information that coach Krzyształowicz came back to Poland after working one year in Manchester City academy. I was extremely excited about the meeting with him. He told me we could meet and work in Warsaw where he was helping his son with one club. I got a chance to work with him individually and with the entire team. I still don't understand that, but no matter what season and mood I can have, I always have the best shape with coach Krzyształowicz. The positive energy is immediately in my mind. During that time, I was really good, and I had a brilliant time working with him in Warsaw. He took care of me during the entire time. I did my best to present myself as great as I could. It was the first time he saw me after our first goalkeeper camp. Before I left, he told me I could play at the highest level in Poland, and he would do his best to help me with that after seeing me during that week. WOW. When I got back home, I had the positive attitude, and I knew that no matter how hard my next season would be with Parasol Wroclaw, I had to work hard to be able to make it to the next level. That was the first time when I was really proud of myself. I knew that I didn't waste my time, and all those situations made me stronger. I just didn't know that the biggest hit was coming.

EIGHT

THE LAST YEAR

The summer before my third year in high school was special for me. First time I was proud of myself when I heard that I made that tremendous growth within two years. Every sacrifice was worth hearing those words once, trust me. However, I told you already that all I needed was a good coach who would care about my progress and success. I could offer all tools, heart and sacrifice to achieve the highest dreams. My ambitions were on another level, but, unfortunately for me, I had to go back to Wroclaw to finish my last year. All I had to do that year was to survive in my team and work hard in my high school to pass everything and graduate. I was waiting for coach Krzyształowicz until he signed his contract with a new team in Poland — it happened quickly. However, I had to wait longer until he got a green light to get a new goalkeeper into the roster. Yeah... I am not patient at all, but I had a huge motivation to make my dreams come true. I put everything I had on the table, and I have learned that, apparently, overworking isn't always paying back with significant results.

Last year in high school is always tough because mature exams are close. All professors are stressed about that, sometimes I think they care more about it than students — especially students from sports programs. All athletes think they don't have to worry about the exams because they will play professionally. I haven't heard anything more stupid than that. Don't be the same athlete as most of your classmates, don't be silly, and take care of the grades. It will be worth it, and I will explain why later.

I always had good grades in my high school. I knew that one of the ways to achieve outstanding success was to be great everywhere, not only on the field. My schedule was very similar to the previous two years. A couple of times during the week, we had to wake up before 6 am, then go to the math class or practice. I hated to wake up so early because it was still very dark outside. It was hard to get myself off the bed when it was rainy and windy outside. After I forced myself to get up, I ate a quick breakfast, and then it was time for school. Between or after the classes I would have my first practice, that was always a pleasure to work with some motivated athletes. Later was a less exciting part of the day, when I had to go to my team practice. I don't even want to talk about it — wasting time. I couldn't afford to waste my time on the free afternoons, so I convinced my mom to let me work individually with a conditioning coach who helped me with my core strength. During the week, every single day I had practices twice a day and games on Saturdays or Sundays. In addition, I was studying every day not only to get good grades, but also to pass the mature exam. Being motivated always helped me to open my books and try to study, but honestly, I don't understand if it was effective at all. My entire body hurt me, so as soon as I got to the bed, I fell asleep only by touching the pillow. Oh, it was the best time of the day. 6 AM, time to wake up again.

My previous decisions didn't matter for me anymore. I had my supreme goal, and I knew what I was working on. Even though I didn't enjoy working out with my current team, I knew that it was my last year, so I wanted to prove that I deserved to be at a better place. I wanted to move forward again. However, there were ups and downs in my games. I had some significant games when I saved everything; I wish I recorded those games. I also had some games where I didn't play my best. Even though I worked harder than ever, I didn't see the major results. I was disappointed about it. After my first year of high school, I lost my wave, and I never found it back while I was playing for Parasol Wroclaw. I wasn't happy after the first part of the season, and my depressive mood after the fall was killing me. At that time, I didn't know that this mood would lead to the explosion inside me.

I hoped that during the winter break I would hear more news about my future. My phone was still quiet, and I had heard nothing from coach Krzyształowicz. I would do everything to receive that call during the winter break, truly everything. I believe that perfect timing is the most important for a lot of athletes to achieve greatness, and, to be honest with you, I have never found that time. I am not sure if you can find it, probably just some athletes get it earlier or later where others might do everything and just never find it. Imagine, on every weekend you are at the regional park from 8am till 12pm, but there is one Saturday when you can't show up because you have to do something important. On the next day, you hear that one random guy was invited for some tryouts and he got a contact of an agent. This unknown guy came to this park for the first time. After you hear this story, you will never skip any weekends at that park. However, this agent will never show up there again. That's how I felt all the time, and that time I was hating everything around because I was pushing myself off the limits, but the good results never came. Rather than getting more motivation to work, I got a hit which almost killed me. Literally, I could be already dead.

I remember that day perfectly. It was a freezing morning, and we had a scrimmage after the winter break. I didn't have to play that game, and I didn't even want to. I was honestly tired after traveling during the break; moreover, I was sick most of my free time. But I still came to the game since I wouldn't feel good if I skipped it. As soon as I got there and saw the snow on the field, I was really disappointed. My character wouldn't let me take a day off, but I really didn't feel that I wanted to play with those conditions. I hoped the game would be cancelled, but I wasn't. I believe that I was the only one goalkeeper who showed up that day, so I was forced to play the entire game on the frozen field. After the game ended, I didn't feel well, and my back hurt me a lot. It was Sunday, so I went to the church in the evening. I had many problems to get up from the bed, but I wanted to go. So, I took a bus, I got there, but I was so weak all the time. After I left the church, I got a weird feeling in my back. I felt like somebody put a knife through my body. I couldn't realize what it was because I was in one piece, but I literally couldn't walk. I got to the dorms and laid down on my bed without any extra moves. I didn't have any painkillers, so I went upstairs to my friends to get some pills. It took me so much time before I got up, and I really had to take a huge break as soon as I came to their door... I got some pills; I took it immediately, hoping I could fall asleep. My best friend, Patryk, was about to come back to the dorms, so I just texted him to bring me more painkillers; otherwise I wouldn't fall asleep. He came to our room and asked what happened, so I told him, "I don't know, but I feel terrible, and my back hurts so much". He gave me some powerful painkiller, and I set my alarm to 6.30am. I had a swimming pool practice that day. My backpack was ready to go, but as soon as I woke up in the morning and couldn't reach my phone to turn the alarm off, I knew that something was wrong. I didn't have any power to go; I stayed at home and called my mom to ask what I should've done. She told me I had to see the doctor. I didn't want to skip my practice and school, but I certainly couldn't move. I listened to her, and I went to the closest hospital...

Do you believe that something can steal all of your dreams in less than one day? Would you agree that some incidents can be the main reason of losing everything you worked on? I am the athlete who knows that all injuries are tough. I always admire athletes who come back after turning ACL. It cannot be easy. Moreover, all minor injuries are difficult too — twisted ankles, pulled muscles, and any other fractures will force an athlete to make some steps back and build the shape from the beginning. But to be honest with you, I don't know if you can face something worse than surgery on your organs. However, I know one thing: it is much worse to face the same pain twice.

Waiting time in the hospital was way too long; I was about to leave and get back to my hometown. I still had time to catch a bus to Zgorzelec. My mom told me to sit and wait for my time to see the doctor. After some time, it was finally my turn. From the beginning, I just did basic exams, and each doctor was touching my chest with a stethoscope. I was pissed at them because I said that my back hurt me, and not my chest. I asked if everything was fine, and if I could leave now. They refused to let me go because there were more things to check. They didn't tell me anything and just sent me to take an RTG picture. As soon as they received the image of my chest, they called a specialist to the office. The primary doctor came and told me that my lung collapsed — we needed to react quickly and put the drainage on. "Wait, what are you talking about? What is drainage, and why do we need to react quickly?", only those thoughts were in my head. I wanted to go home, but the doctor said that he couldn't let me leave the hospital without helping me out. If I had waited longer, I would have had two collapsed lungs instead of one. In that case, I wouldn't be able to catch a breath, and I could die. He told me I had to sign some papers to allow them to do their job. Before I signed any paper, I asked when I would be able to come back on the field; the doctor was quiet and didn't say a word to me. Imagine if I had tried to catch that bus to go home because I wasn't patient to wait... I called my mom, and explained the whole situation. I think it terrified her, and she didn't wait long to come visit me with my grandparents. I also called Patryk and told him I might've had to stay in the hospital for the next few days, so I would need to get some clothes from my room. I told him to wait until I would be done with some drainage, but I didn't really know what it was. After I was done with talking, the doctor called me to his office again to explain the next steps. He didn't mention anything specific except that the procedure could be a little painful. They took me to the special room where everything was already prepared. I got an injection with a painkiller, but it didn't work at all. They got through my ribs in my chest to place a special tube inside it. With this drainage my lung was supposed to get to the normal size, and I was supposed to leave the hospital after a few days. Of course, the machine didn't work well, and with every move of the stupid tube, the pain was reaching the highest grade which was 10. My family and my room-mate were worrying about me because I looked like a ghost after taking all those pills. I had to take them to lower the pain.

Everyone was worrying about my health while I was worrying about my soccer career. As soon as my mom got to the hospital, I asked her to talk with the doctor about my future on the field. She said that she tried, but the doctor wanted to talk with me tomorrow in person. I already knew something was wrong. With my pain, I couldn't fall asleep, I couldn't move and turn, I couldn't collect all my thoughts because for the first time I saw the end in the tunnel without the happy ending.

I didn't sleep during the first night, I just couldn't do it. I was extremely surprised when around 4 am I saw some people walking around the hall and getting coffee. I thought they were crazy. Later, I understood that they couldn't sleep because their health was even worse than mine. When the morning came, I couldn't wait to see my doctor to hear some news about my health. He came as he promised, but rather than talking about the important stuff for me, he was asking what I did before and tried to explain why collapse happened to me. I was lost because I didn't worry why; I worried about what's next. Finally, after a few days of bothering him about my soccer career, he told me it would be good for me if I invested my time in something else rather than sport because I would never be able to come back to the field again. That was the toughest talk I had ever had so far.

Before I couldn't sleep because of the pain, and later, I couldn't sleep because I was a prisoner of my own thoughts. How could I do something different? That's impossible. Maybe the doctor just made a mistake. Everyone was trying to calm me down, they were telling me to be focused on getting to the normal shape first.

It's easy to say to forget about something, but it is hard to really do it. I believe the toughest part for the athletes is that we don't have other hobbies while investing our whole time in sport. We just don't have time to meet other friends than the ones from the field. Even though we can be good at school, we might not have a plan B which is necessary. I just wish you would never have to experience that on your own, but understand one thing — being focused only on sport is not always the best investment.

I didn't want to believe in that, and I couldn't forget about soccer. I didn't want to talk with anyone about that, but I knew that I would come back on the field. I just had to get out from the hospital and get some recovery time. After one week, doctors told me that in the next few days I could leave. I felt that I struggled with my condition and walking, but I thought it was because of the drainage. Even though I was nervous, I couldn't wait for the doctors to take it out. After they did that, it hurt me so badly for a few minutes, and it was so weird to breathe normally again. I was so happy that I got through that time; however, when I took the first few steps, I was extremely tired and had to sit down to catch a breath. Before we got to the car with my family, I had to find a couple of benches on the way. I didn't have a good condition at all; moreover, I was in panic because I never felt like that before.

All I was worrying about was my school. I wasn't able to attend it for the next few weeks, but professors offered me plenty of help — I got some homework to do at home and an extension for some assignments. I felt alone and lost since my "fast" living changed, and I couldn't do anything about it. Even my tough grandfather wasn't bad for me anymore, and all our talks were very polite; however, without mentioning any sport or competition. I knew that my family was worrying about me, but my grandmother, Dorota, was optimistic and was giving me some hopes. She turned that time into a positive experience and told me to find something I liked to do except sport. Yes, that was very tough, and actually I found nothing back then. I convinced my grandfather to give me some driving lessons because I really had nothing to do. In addition, I was doing my homework and preparing for mature exams, but I couldn't stay home any longer, so I asked if I could go back to the school again. Everyone agreed for my return, but I had to follow some restrictions — I had to be really careful and wasn't allowed to lift anything.

All my classmates helped me with everything they possibly could, I didn't even have to carry my backpack. It was good to be back in school, but I was so sad and jealous while I was watching my friends during the practices. I wanted to be with them on the field. Every coach from SMS talked with me, but I didn't want to complain and tell the truth, so I said that I hoped to come back to the field shortly. I was following all the restrictions, working on my grades, and getting used to the reality. I was thinking about my grandmother's advice, and I signed up for a driving license's course. First time in my life I had plenty of time after classes. I remember that after I did my theory practice, I had my first lesson in the car. I thought the lesson would be like those with my grandfather. However, rather than driving on the parking lot, my instructor took me immediately on the road. I was nervous, but I did it — I survived my first real driving lesson. I had to make 30 hours before I could take a practice test and go to the state exam. It was fun, and I got involved in learning how to drive. I was supposed to finish my lessons shortly, but one day when I was walking back to the dorms from the school, I got the same pain on my back. I felt like a knife was getting through my chest again. The doctor mentioned before that I could feel some similar pain; I knew that my lung collapsed again. I really struggled with walking those last meters to the dorms, and when I got there, everyone knew that it happened again. They were about to call the ambulance, but I said that I would go to the hospital on my own — I couldn't be more stupid, but that's who I was back then. I always had to do something in my own way. Even though I knew that everything was happening again, my friend and I took a taxi to the hospital where I had to wait for a long time before my doctor saw me. I went directly to his office and told him that my lung collapsed again, but rather than getting some help, he told me to go through the whole procedure. So, I spent a few hours waiting for the drainage.

Before, I was told that everything was fine with my lungs; however, I wasn't even thinking about coming on the field yet. I knew it was far away from me, but I didn't know the consequences when my lung collapsed for the second time. That time I had to have a surgery; otherwise, it would be too risky, and my lung would collapse again and again. I was depressed, and I lost all my tiny hopes of getting back to the field ever again. That event was much worse and caused me much more pain than the first collapse. I was told that my chest had to be open to make some necessary moves. If they did that, I would never be able to compete at any level.

I was supposed to have the surgery before the weekend, but somehow, they had to move my surgery for another day. During the weekend, most doctors didn't work at that section of the hospital. I was just waiting for my day; in the meantime, I was watching older people after the heart attack — they had opened chests. I was extremely worried about it because at the age of 18 I didn't want to have a chest like that. With no hopes, I was just lying in my bed and waiting to feel better. In the morning, I got a phone call from my mom; she told me she would transfer me to another hospital which specialized on lung-related problems. I knew that if my mom wanted to do something, she would get to talk with the president within a few hours. She did everything, and on the day when my chest was supposed to be open, we changed the hospital. Everything went nicely, and doctors were planning the laser surgery. My mom did something huge for me, she saved my future.

In that hospital, I was getting morphine. This drug works very effectively on pain. The whole surgery went successfully. As soon as I opened my eyes for the first time, I saw my mom and grandfather outside my recovery room. Later, I saw that my father came from London to support me too. That time was hard for everyone. I remember the first day after the surgery. The physiotherapist came and forced me to do some exercises. I thought he was crazy because I couldn't even wear underpants on my own, and he told me to move my arms up and down. I was shocked, but without him, I would just lay on that bed and think about the pain rather than recovery. The best part of each day in the hospital was working out with physiotherapists. I felt much better, but I was weak and tired even after going to the bathroom. My shape was getting better, so I was lowered on morphine. After the next few days, they told me I was ready to go home.

I thought that I got through my pain and nasty times. But awful times just came when I literally didn't have any condition. After spending plenty of time lying with a sort of new lung, I could walk only for 2 minutes, but then I had to sit for 5 minutes or longer to catch some breath. I didn't think about playing sports, but I was worrying about my mature exams. If I didn't pass them, I wouldn't be able to go to college. Even though I didn't have plan B, I knew that no matter what I had to pass those exams. My professors helped me and let me prepare for the exams on my own. With that being said, I created my own routine with studying each subject, so I felt truly prepared to pass those exams. In addition, I added some workouts to my routine. First, I started with some stretching by the wall and walked around the kitchen. Few days later, I could make my first walk around the house. I was so proud because I could see the results of my work. Next, I was able to make a longer walk around the neighborhood. I was walking often because only then I could be focused on myself while listening to music. My whole family was worrying about me, even my grandparents were against the idea of coming back to sport. Being a prisoner of my own thoughts at that time wasn't easy, but I was getting close to forgive myself and quit playing soccer…

One day, my mom called me because she had something important to tell me. She didn't want to talk by the phone, so I was waiting for her at home. When she got back, I couldn't wait to listen to her thoughts. She asked if coach Krzyształowicz called me yet, and I said that I didn't get anything, so she told me to expect a call from him. I was super surprised and thought that he probably just wanted to tell me something like, "Everything will be fine, you will find other hobbies than being a goalkeeper". To be honest with you, these words would help me a lot. Every time when he was talking with me, I got better immediately.

The next day, I was in the house with my grandmother and siblings, playing some games. Finally, I got the call from coach Krzyształowicz, so I went outside to the back of the house. I was expecting words similar to "everything will be alright, you are a talented kid, you can find something else", but I couldn't believe my ears after what I heard. He told me that he got a green light to get a new goalkeeper into Lech Poznań. What, excuse me? I didn't know what to say. I was completely out of words since I was getting peace with myself of quitting soccer for real after the surgery. He told me he was giving me some time because he knew about my shape and everything I had to go through from my mom. Later, she explained me that she got a call from coach Krzyształowicz while she was at work. Coach told her he would like to invite me for official tryouts to one of the best teams in Poland. My mom wasn't able to talk, and only when she could say a few words, she told him that he called in the really bad time because I was praying for that phone call since our last meeting in Warsaw during the summer. The conversation was hard for them, but coach Krzyształowicz wasn't scared to call me with the big news. I hope now you understand that some athletes can never find the perfect timing. I was very close to say goodbye to the ball, and then this one call changed my future.

After that call I started to walk more than once per day. I wanted to push myself and get back to the shape. After some time, I could already jog a little. Slowly I was getting back to be ready to run for a few minutes. I took it seriously, but I promised my family that now I would be careful. I didn't want to force anything because I knew that, even with my huge attitude, I just might not be able to come back on the competitive field again. Everyone was calming me down because they didn't want me to have big hopes since I was already disappointed enough. Without the hope everything would be dark, but I had something to think about. In the meantime, it was time for mature exams — my unknown plan

B was about to start. I graduated from high school with some awards, but most importantly, some professors and coaches were stopping my mom and grandfather in the hall to tell that I was a special person with amazing determination to work. All of them said that my relatives could be really proud of me, and they were.

LITTLE NOTE for everyone from SMS Junior Wroclaw:

"I wanted to thank everyone who had an enormous impact on making my high school years absolutely special. To all my classmates who made this class highly competitive, but, at the same time, formed the most enjoyable environment to be a part of. I wanted to say big thanks especially to my roommate and my best friend Patryk Biegański, who survived three years in one room with me. Also, big appreciation to all coaches, such as Ryszard Pietraszewski (the head coach), Janusz Jedynak (GK coach during the first and the second years), Jarosław Muracki and Artur Wozniak (TGK TEAM, GK coaches during the third year), who created the best possible program for me to develop during those three years. Lastly, big gratitude to all my professors and directors, such as Mirosław Łyszczak (the head professor of our class), Janusz Siepietowski (the sport director), Grzegorz Kalinkiewicz (the director of our school), and Anna Tymińska-Bella (the president of the school) since

without them nothing would be possible, and I could never continue my future education. Even though at that time we didn't understand what they were trying to do, they took care of our future, and for that heads off. Thanks to all of you!"

NINE

MENTORING PART 2

LECH POZNAŃ TRYOUTS

How big are your dreams? Would you be able to describe your daydreams? Where would you like to play and why? With whom would you like to work, what is the principal reason for that? What facilities would you like to have? Would you rather have the contract with Nike, Adidas, or another brand? Is the money really the most important? What makes you happy? Do you see your future as an elite athlete? Please close your eyes and try to answer for these or even more questions.

When you are done with your answers, here are my own:

I've always wanted to play at the highest level — no matter what, that is my dream. To be more specific, I want to play in the premier league; however, I would love to be a part of a professional team anywhere. My dreams are very simple — signing my first contract with a professional team, being the starter, and winning the championship with them, maybe a couple of times. I want to play somewhere where I don't have to worry about my recovery equipment, such as swimming pools, jacuzzis, massages, etc. I would admire to have a great coaching staff, and, to be more specific, I want to be a part of the team where coach Krzyształowicz will work with me every day. In addition, being a part of a team where I wouldn't worry about injuring myself because of the bad quality facilities is more than enough to make me feel great. I know that coach Krzyształowicz will prepare me to play at another level. With him, I am constantly in the best shape because of his work ethic and experience. He knows how to get the best of me, and that's why I want to be a part of his roster.

I would choose to play in a big stadium with plenty of fields around, so with each practice I can feel the atmosphere of coming to work and getting ready to play the official game. To be honest with you, I don't care about the brand, I will be grateful for getting free equipment for the entire season. The money was never the crucial part of getting me into soccer, but I know that I would prefer to be treated fairly. Moreover, I would love to be a part of a team who knows how to manage the locker room and the relationships inside it. I definitely see my future as a good athlete, and I would do my best to be a great one.

I am opening my eyes, and here we are, I am inside the locker room in Lech Poznań.

As I promised my family and myself, that time I had to be very careful with getting back to the field. I couldn't afford to have the same troubles with my health again. I put a lot of effort into practices. Walking, jogging, and later running were the key parts of my daily schedule. I did a lot of mobility exercises; I touched the ball a couple of times, but I was scared to dive yet, and I wasn't able to face that fear. Moreover, I didn't play as a goalkeeper for a long time. All doctors told me that most likely I would never come back to the field again. I wanted to prove that they were all wrong. That was my major motivation through every single practice with my shade.

The easiest part for all athletes is to work hard when somebody is watching and supporting them, but one of the hardest parts is to do the same thing when you are all alone. I was completely alone with that because everyone was scared to help me with trainings — in their minds, I wasn't supposed to practice at all.

I was used to do it before, so even that time I really enjoyed it — I was my own boss. Even though nothing was sure, I had some hopes and really didn't want to waste my last chance of playing soccer. That one call changed my attitude, and from lying at home, complaining about everything around, I believed in myself and moved from the bed. I worked regularly and could run very well within 3 months after the surgery — my condition had improved a lot. However, I didn't touch the ground as a goalkeeper even once. I was scared, and I wasn't certain if I could break that dread.

One day in July, I got a call from coach Krzyształowicz who asked about my shape. I remember that he asked me how I felt, and if I got back to the field already. Of course, I had to lie because I didn't want to lose my opportunity of coming for big tryouts, so I said that I felt great and already got a chance to be at the field as a goalkeeper. I couldn't be more stupid than that. I risked my coach's reputation because he was responsible for bringing top-class goalkeepers to the first team. What is more, I risked my own health and, at the same time, the last chance of playing. I wasn't able to understand that I could say the truth and just wait a little longer. However, back then, I wasn't capable of breaking that fear of diving, so I figured it was the best choice. With that being said, coach Krzyształowicz told me that Lech Poznań was completing my official invitation for the tryouts, so I just had to wait for the official starting time. Tryouts were going to be for a couple of days. In the meantime, I could watch and support the team since they played qualifications for UEFA Champions League, the most important tournament for soccer clubs. I got some snacks and enjoyed the game. I was also learning the names because I didn't know most of the players in Lech Poznań.

Right after I finished watching them live on TV, I got the message that I had to check in on the next day. I took the first available train to Poznań and arrived in the early morning. As soon as I got there, coach Krzyształowicz met me by the stadium and showed me everything around. I was able to get some breakfast with the top athletes who were just playing in one of the most important tournaments in the world. That was an extremely cool experience, but I didn't want to get too excited and lose my mind. I was introduced to everyone, and for the first time in my life I was finally in my dream.

Coach Krzyształowicz organized everything for me — I could even be with the team in the locker room, which is very rare these days. I was extremely lucky because most of the times the club wouldn't allow anyone to sit in their locker room. After breakfast, we had some free time, so I could make friends and experience how nice it was to have their lives. All the players received new Nike cleats, and the funniest thing was that almost nobody liked them because they were pink. I took a quick run to the main stadium, which could fit over 43 thousand people during the game. Can you believe it? But it wasn't the biggest impression yet. Around 10.30

am we left to the practice. I had never been on the better grass before, I could even sleep there, that's how soft it was. Moreover, the second and third goalkeeper, who I was about to have practice with, said that the grass was too dry, so the coach went to turn on the water before practice started. Yeah... I was super scared because I didn't know if I could face my fear and collapse on that soft grass for the first time in 5 months.

Getting ready for a practice had never been that easy. A lot of people were helping me out; for example, some people carried my equipment to the field, others were giving me my practice jersey. Also, the drinks for each player were already made and I could find them next to the goal. The field was prepared for every practice; the grass was wet, so the ball moved way faster than I have ever experienced before.

When we all went to the field, people walking in front of me played for the national teams, so I couldn't be selfish and think about my fear of diving. The whistle was blown, and all players had to go to their stations. Of course, goalkeepers went to work with coach Krzysz-tałowicz. He talked a little about the last game, and then we moved to our practice. During the first drill we were working on the goalkeeper position with diving at the same time. As soon as I touched the ball, I overcame my fear of diving. Believe me or not, but after 5 months of stretching and running, I was able to make my first dive.

I smelled the ground for the first time in Lech and completely forgot that I was injured — I was flying immediately. That time I wasn't a kid who was hitting the ground, I was the man who was literally flying in the air.

The whole practice went excellent, and I was so surprised about dealing with the fear of diving. I felt like it was gone as soon as I had a chance to work with the coach and his team. I didn't have time to think about how to dive, I just never forgot about it — everything was waiting for the right moment inside me. I felt wonderful, and after the practice some kids came from behind the fence and asked us for autographs. I answered them that I wasn't playing there yet. They said that they saw me during the practice, and they were sure about my career with Lech. It was a pleasure for me to talk with the kids who were so excited about talking with the first team. After the practice, coach Krzyształowicz told me that Marcin Robak, the current forward of Lech Poznań, would take care of me since he was staying at the same hotel with his family. So, whenever he was ready to leave the stadium, I packed my stuff and was ready to go. We were staying in a pleasant hotel nearby the stadium. To every practice I would come with the Lech's top player. Am I bragging too much?

I had a pleasure to train with the first goalkeeper, Jasmin Burić. I will never forget his advice. He was extremely polite and was the one who showed me how to kick the ball through the entire field. In addition, I had practice with Krzysztof Kotorowski, one of the most important goalkeepers in Lech Poznań for many years. I remember that I was doing minimum 10 repetitions of every drill while he was doing only two or three just to keep the shape. After years, I understand what the differences between young and older athletes at the highest level are. Furthermore, coach Krzyształowicz made a competition between me and the second goalkeeper at that time, Maciej Gostomski, one of the funniest guys in the locker room, and I won it. I even forgot that I had a surgery a couple of months ago. My mind was there, but my body wasn't yet — I was struggling with recovering time. Overall, I was proud of myself, and I thought I made a great impression on coaching staff.

At the end of my tryouts I had two last things to do. I had a meeting with the team doctor and one game to watch against Lechia Gdańsk. First on that day, my goalkeeper coach and I went to meet with the doctor. I was sure that I presented myself strongly enough to stay over there, especially with my quick progress after the injury. It would be a very prospective move to make; however, the doctor saw things differently. I couldn't believe my ears, and I saw that my coach was surprised too. Rather than saying some positives about my progress within a few months, the doctor said that I shouldn't have been there, and it was a huge risk to put me on the field. I couldn't be more shocked because I knew my body — I was the one who got myself in shape from having the tube inside my chest. I could compete at the top level again, all I needed was just to work with a strength conditioning coach who would prepare my body for that, and Lech Poznań could provide me that service and get me to the next level. My coach was standing there like a ghost. He asked if there were any chances to check me out with some medical exams, but the doctor said that it would take some time before we could move forward with my paperwork. I knew that something went wrong, and I was pissed about the doctor's opinion because he made a huge mistake by following just the standard procedure with me. I wasn't some random guy; I was a kid who had nothing to lose, and the biggest dreams were in front of me. Coach Krzyształowicz told me he would find out about the possibilities for me, but I felt that he wasn't sure. I knew him closely, so I could feel it. I didn't have a great mood while going to the game and sitting on VIP spot. Rather than watching the game and having fun, I was thinking about how nice it was if I could be there and offer those seats to my family and friends. Lech Poznań won that game 2:1 against Lechia Gdańsk. I was so proud to be a part of the blue family and hoped that the coach would find some options to get me to the roster.

On the next day, it was time to check out from the hotel and get back home, back to the sad reality where life didn't have any taste. I was praying for working with somebody who would really take care of me. I knew that I was on the perfect way to recover from something that most people wouldn't even take a shot of getting back from. I had a train to Wroclaw around 1pm. I had to wait to hear something more from my coach, but I had grim feelings about it.

As soon as I arrived in Wroclaw, I talked with my family and friends because I wanted to tell them everything. They didn't believe me at all, most of them didn't even know that I went to Lech Poznań. I didn't like to talk about it too much; I was focused on getting the job done. One day, I got a call from coach Krzyształowicz who told me that unfortunately we couldn't move forward with getting me into the first team. They had to get a goalkeeper who was able to compete at any time, and I wasn't able to do that. I was super sad about it, but with time I understood what he was talking about. Shortly, the first goalkeeper got injured. So, the second goalkeeper made it to the goal, and the third one was sitting on the bench. If something happened to the current starter, I would already be on the bench with one of the best teams in Poland. I couldn't cheat myself, I wasn't there yet, but I knew that I would make it quickly. I just had to get a chance.

I was working hard to get to the right place, but I wasn't able to make it at the perfect time. As you can see, finding the perfect timing hasn't been for me. Till today I wonder what would have happened if I had got a chance to be under steady observation of the first team in Lech Poznań and just to play most of the games with their second team. I really believe that today I wouldn't have to worry about my next steps in the soccer career. I knew my body, and I knew that the doctor wasn't right with telling me that I couldn't be eligible to participate. All I had to get was someone who would do the basics with me, and coach Krzyształowicz could prepare me quickly to reach that level. Back then, I didn't get that chance, but I cannot complain at all. I have experienced something that most people wouldn't even be close to, and that's why I was and still am proud of myself.

Coach Krzyształowicz mentioned that he would follow my career and we would be in touch with my next steps. For a long time, I haven't seen the same quality services after I left Lech Poznań. I got a chance to perform for Pogoń Oleśnica, 4th division back then, where Ryszard Pietraszewski was the head coach. It was a good level for me to develop in the senior team. The most important thing for me was being there with no pressure of rushing my comeback to the field, so I could take my time preparing my shape to play again. However, I just didn't know how smart coach Krzyształowicz was with not getting me into the first team because of my shape problems. In addition, I wanted to prove that everyone around was wrong, so rather than taking my time, I was rushing to get back to the field and hoping to receive the next call from him.

When you are injured, you need to learn to be very patient. Trust me, I am the one who can give you some advice — rushing to come back is the dumbest thing you can do. Especially when other people offer you plenty of help. When they ask you if something hurts, don't hide it and don't be a hero, don't be selfish and think about the responsibilities and ultimate results. Rather than having some benefits of getting to the field quick enough, such as playing a big game or being on important tryouts, think about the effects. Everyone who tried to help you could get fired only because you were greedy by hiding the truth with your pain and your health. I know that they taught you to do that, but when you are in a good position at the highest level, you don't have to be the tiger anymore — at that level your health is the priority since only with great health you perform your best. Be smart, and smartness in that scenario shows in coming back on the field when you are 110% ready to play again. Perform your best, and bigger benefits will come.

LITTLE NOTE FOR COACH KRZYSZTAŁOWICZ:

"Coach, to begin with this message, I wanted to apologize about lying to you about my shape. I am sorry, but if I hadn't lied, I would have felt like my chance would be gone. I didn't want to let it go, I needed it so badly. This chance meant for me more than anything else in soccer. I could see my dream, I could touch it, and I could be a part of it. In addition, you helped me with facing the biggest fear which was diving back then. I bet that right now you are extremely surprised how I performed back then without touching the ground for a long time before the tryouts days. Even though it didn't work out, you gave me a chance to hope and believe again that I belong to that level. Please, never think you are the major reason who put me into a prison of my own thoughts. You are the one who gave me the key to answer for many questions during the most troublesome times in my life. Next, I wanted to thank you for literally every-thing what you did for me. You kicked my ass and pushed me to believe that I could still achieve something great. This one call when you told me about your green light changed everything. From that day, I forgot that I was injured. You gave me my dream back, and I was close to make it happen. However, you just offered me very limited time to make it achievable. Just kidding. I did my best to make you proud. THANK YOU!"

TEN

RUSHING BACK

The worst point for all athletes is that they have to sacrifice practically their entire life to get a chance to be seen on the field. I met some friends who didn't even graduate high school, but most of the time, they never cared about their education. With this attitude, most athletes in Europe struggle with taking the challenge of enrolling to colleges. Education in Poland is for free; however, people need to get good scores from mature exams and a good final GPA from high school. Based on that, universities in Poland decide about accepting students into the program. Even though I didn't agree with the doctor's opinion, I enrolled at Pogoń Oleśnica, but at the same time, I had to start my education path at the university level like I promised to my family. They told me I had to have a plan B, which was getting a degree in higher education back then.

The season in Pogoń Oleśnica was depressing for me. My shape was terrible. Overall, I wasn't able to take a part in most of the practices and games. Coach Krzyształowicz was right with not signing the contract with me. It would be too risky for both of us; however, with their services I had a better opportunity to recover. Oleśnica offered me a lot of support, and I didn't have to rush with coming back to the field. I wasn't patient back then, and I wanted to check if my body was ready to fly again. My game appearances weren't regular at all, during fall I could play only 3 games out of 15. With that being said, I spent most of fall and winter seasons inside the gym, working out with our strength conditioning coach. He was supposed to prepare me to come back in spring. He did a magnificent job and was the first one who wasn't scared of helping me out. However, even with his help, it wasn't enough to get me ready to play again, and during spring I could play only in 4 games out of 15. In the meantime, I had problems with breathing a few times, but luckily for me, my lung didn't collapse the third time. Coming back and playing was getting harder for me, so I had to stop risking my health. I made the decision that I wouldn't go back to Pogoń Oleśnica for the next season. However, I wanted to check myself somewhere else.

The toughest part of deciding is to be aware of the

consequences. I didn't have my own plan B. I had to make a crucial decision, and my soccer career wasn't clear without me playing in Pogoń Oleśnica next year. In the meantime, I wanted to find some new hobbies. Otherwise, I would repeatedly be a prisoner of my own thoughts with looking for the answer if I still wanted to play soccer. Did I want to? I couldn't answer that. After the season ended, I said that I would not return for the next one. When I was asked why, I simply answered: I didn't see the future with soccer in Pogoń Oleśnica.

In addition, it was my first year in college. I was looking for new hobbies to get an idea about my future career. I met many friends, and it was the first time when I had contact with people outside of soccer. It was strange, and I couldn't get used to it. I couldn't believe my ears when everyone was introducing themselves at our first gym class. Our major was Sport Management, and it was Physical Education University, yet most of the people have never participated in any sport. That was a vast change in my life because people had much different topics and interests than me. Finally, it was time to shine with something different from soccer. Furthermore, adjusting from the high school system, where professors were reminding us about the due dates and helping us out to pass the exams, to the university, where professors told us the requirements only once, was very hard from the beginning for me. As a rookie, I had some problems with following the due dates, but my friends and I always helped each other with it. All of us thought the mature exams were really hard to pass. But as soon as our first finals came, we all understood that mature exams were nothing compared to the finals from anatomy and other university classes.

College life has many advantages, but you have to learn how to manage that. The parties are dominant and meeting new friends is priceless. However, it is easy to lose yourself and get nasty habits with partying too much. That might be the crucial reason for failing all the classes. Trust me, professors will never run to help you out, so it is your responsibility to take care of the business. It was a tremendous challenge for me, but at the end of the day, learning how to follow directions correctly has been very important in my life. I passed everything; however, I wasn't sure if I would come back for the second year.

ELEVEN

THE REALITY

I was looking for the last better chance to play, so I went to try myself in England. I went for open tryouts and met the coach, Billy Stewart, who was the head goalkeeper coach in the Accrington Stanley. Back then, they played in League Two division, which was a very high level. Within two years, they earned the spot at the higher level, League One. It could be the chance for my dream to come true again. I was waiting for the invitation from coach Stewart, so I tried to keep myself in the best possible shape. One day, Stewart called me and invited me for the tryouts. I had to get there and pay for everything on my own, such as for a place to stay and food. I didn't like it, but I didn't have a choice. That was my last shot.

British English was hard for me to understand, and

back then, I didn't speak English at all. I took a bus and went to Accrington, United Kingdom. I was familiar with London and really liked the speed of living over there. However, when I saw the compact city, Accrington, I wanted to leave that place as soon as I found my apartment. The city was reminding me of a huge village where you had to walk for a long time to see some people, and I didn't like it. Finally, I met my coach who showed me my room. I didn't understand him at all, but I believed that he was telling me to get ready for tomorrow's practice. I told my dad to call him and ask about everything. I really couldn't understand any words, and I was completely alone somewhere in the United Kingdom. It was tough.

I got to the locker room with huge expectations after spending some time in Lech Poznań. I heard that soccer in the UK has the most money, so I was hoping to see better facilities than Lech had. I couldn't be more wrong. The stadium was so tiny, very similar to Pogoń Oleśnica, and training facilities were placed near the stadium. However, it differed from Lech's facilities since they didn't have the same security needs. The only good thing was the grass — they took fantastic care of it, so the ball was moving quickly. I didn't understand anyone in the locker room, but, for my benefit, most of the players were sitting only on their phones until the practice came.

We went for our first practice; I had a pleasure to

work with the first team where the youngest goalkeeper was around 26 years old. Back then, I was only 19. Our technique abilities were on the similar level; however, as soon as we got to work with the team, they had time to shine since they had more experience with playing at that stage. The ball was moving quickly and with vast power. Sometimes, I thought a shot would literally break my arm, but I didn't even have time to react — I was praying to not get hit by that ball. Moreover, while we were playing the games, all players were fighting for survival. They wouldn't step back and let one ball go out. If they had to go hard on you, they would slice with straight legs to make you feel pain. Even though most of the players had some good contracts, they all wanted to achieve more and get into the next levels — only a few levels left to greatness. In result, they had to fight hard for everything because only the best and the toughest could play at that standard. One time during the practice my defender got hit, and he was lying on the ground for a long time. Other players didn't even stop the play until they scored the goal. After that, they went to check if the defender was fine. I think he had to leave the field for a little, but soon enough, he came back.

That time, my tryouts differed from Lech Poznań's ones. It was in a different country, so there were different rules. The reality of playing soccer in the UK wasn't like in my dream. Even though I would do my best to play at the premier league level before, I wasn't even sure if it was worth it at that time. I was sitting on the main field, and for the first time in my life I had a talk with myself about everything I had gone through to get to that place. I wasn't even sure if the ultimate prize would be worth all my sacrifices — even the spot in Accrington Stanley wasn't able to pay me back. I was lost in my own thoughts, and as a prisoner I couldn't find the answer if I still wanted to play soccer.

They didn't sign the contract with me because I didn't speak English at all. That was the first time when I felt very dumb. The head coach was yelling at me to kick the ball long, but I didn't understand and was passing the ball for a few yards. When he wanted me to start short, I thought he meant long, so I sent the ball to the forwards. He was getting mad at me regularly, so the goalkeeper coach told me that unfortunately they didn't know how to communicate with me back then. I got back to my dad's house in London and finally felt free of looking for the answer to my favorite question — "Do I really want this?" No, I didn't want it back then. I gave up my dreams and found peace with it. It was time for me to come back for my second year and find something different from kicking the ball.

TWELVE

HOBBIES

B eing an elite athlete with a big future is worth everything — trust me. However, everyone needs to meet some difficulties, and no matter what, some athletes cannot push themselves through these times on the way to greatness. As soon as you make it to the place you want to be at, you can replay the voices in your head with all the advice you heard before. Do your best to have good grades, go to college, and get a degree because it's necessary nowadays. Without having influential people around, you would close your future with sports dreams. Don't be foolish and take some notes on what others, more experienced people, have to say about life. However, don't you ever let others steal your dreams. You need to learn how to get benefits in life without giving up anything what belongs to you. Let me save your time and give the answer for the life test — be passionate about life and have more hobbies than only sport. It's very easy to say, but harder than ever to do it. Good luck with that.

My family was consistently giving me excellent advice, and I was lucky that I didn't give up my education. Back then, I wasn't sure if my major was right for me, but I knew that I had to keep searching for something I would put my heart into again. For a long time, I didn't see any brightness in my future. I just stopped playing soccer, so slowly I got out of soccer language, but I was poor without it. Rather than going every day to practice on the field, I was working in the weight room a few times per week. I kept my pleasant habits, but my lifestyle changed a lot. From the beginning, I liked it because I didn't have any obligations — I was my own boss. Finally, I had more time for my friends, and I didn't have to say "no" when we were heading to a party. It was fun, and I really had an enjoyable time with all of them.

One day, when I was coming back from the party, I was just a little drunk when I had another talk in my own prison. I was asking myself if that was the path I wanted to choose. Before I answered that, I could see my entire life, and how I was always trying to get rid of the bad habits. I didn't party at all and was focused only on doing something great. Looking for other hobbies became hard for me, and I didn't deal well with it. I couldn't forgive myself for giving up my dreams for something worthless. After some time, I was ready to answer, and I said to myself that it was time to stop partying. Instead, it was time to start thinking about my future. I could leave the prison and be focused on my next steps.

In the meantime, my friends and I traveled a lot. We had some glorious trips without planning them at all. One of the biggest advantages of studying in college is your free time between the semesters. If you pass the finals on the first day, you have more than enough time to rest between the terms. After the finals, I was sitting at home and checking the tickets on Skyscanner. I just had nothing else to do, and that day I saw super cheap tickets to Rome. Without wasting time, I texted all my friends who could be interested in making that trip with me. One of my best buddies since college, Lukasz Galik, wasn't able to make it, but Jan Wawrzyniak didn't have to think long about the upcoming trip. When we saw the prices, we were just thinking about how low they were, but we forgot to check our wallets carefully. We landed in Rome and found the hostel. Waiting in the line to get one of the best espressos near Pantheon or eating the best Italian pizza from a street store helped me with finding another hobby. While we were at Rome, I started my first blog — gorszczaromania (https://gorszczaromania.wordpress.-com). I wrote everything about Rome. Even though my skills to write haven't been that good in Polish, it was the beginning of my new passion. Traveling, reading, writing, and finding passions in daily life became my new hobbies. Overall, I was looking for the best adventures.

I always remembered that my dad and I won the green card lottery. However, most of my friends didn't even know about it until summer started. I was always told that the United States offered many possibilities for athletes. I also knew that education there was way too expensive for me, and I wasn't able to pay for the tuition with no athletic scholarship money. In addition, my uncle and I had a great talk one day — he told me to be involved in something that I was good at, and I didn't have to be the greatest. I said that I could get some benefits only from soccer, but I wasn't thinking about it seriously — back then, I thought it was too late for me to become a pro player. He agreed with me and helped with finding some chances to perform. A few days later, I texted my goalkeeper coach from Total Goalkeeping, Jarosław Muracki, and asked him if we could meet and talk about my solid future plans.

I didn't have to think a lot about organizing everything around, but I needed somebody's help. Coach Muracki and whole Total Goalkeeping team could help me with everything. We met at my college; we were sitting in the cafeteria and talking for a long time. One of the principal things of our talk was getting me back into goalkeeper practices; however, I told him not to spread the news around all coaches because I wasn't sure if my idea would even work. I had a break from soccer for less than one year, so I wanted to see if my mood and hunger to play came back. If you want to achieve greatness, one of the ways to do that is to find the happiness of doing little things on the way of getting the main prize.

I felt ready to be on the field, but I didn't want to participate in a lot of goalkeeper practices. I was working out at the gym to get my core ready to be at the field and also added one goalkeeper practice per week. My first practice showed me I could use my experience in many ways. One of the prime ways was to prepare myself to fly in the air again. It wasn't the easiest part for me because everyone was much better from the beginning. Sooner than later, my shape was getting better, so I asked for more goalkeeper practices.

Finally, I could work on the field every day without having any troubles. My body was ready; moreover, my mind was in the right place. I didn't think too much about playing again, so I just enjoyed the moment of being on the goal. At the same time, I took care of my second year in college. I passed all my classes and started to prepare for the finals. One day, my dad called me and asked if we were moving forward with the green card process. I was silent for a bit and didn't know what to say. I told him that I needed some time to think about it. I found happiness, but I was curious about the new challenge. Finally, it was time to talk with my family and friends. Everyone was shocked and excited about my alternative possibility. My family told me I had their full support, but the decision itself I had to make on my own. Of course, my closest friends didn't want me to leave, but at the end of our talk, they told me I should go no matter what. I knew that they didn't believe in most of my plans, but they wanted me to experience something else in life rather than just studying in Poland. Even though I heard lots of positives about going to the United States, I saw plenty of disadvantages of that choice at the same time. I wasn't ready to leave all my family, friends, and current life; on the other hand, I wasn't able to say no to my dad. As a result, I was playing poker with everyone — my dad, family, friends, and even with myself — I didn't know what next cards would be, nobody could predict it.

Summer was getting closer, and my dad and I had to move forward with the green card process steps. It was stressful not only because of my exams, but also because of the pressure of making a really important decision. I passed all the finals, and later, we had a mandatory camp in our college. I was so close to earn my bachelor's degree — I was missing less than a year, but at the same time, I wasn't 100% sure what to do with it.

Of course, I was thinking about my summertime

because I wanted to get rid of that pressure above my head. First, I had my college camp — even though it wasn't nice to wake up at 7 am during the summer or after the parties (name it on your own), it was a marvelous time! Next, I had a goalkeeper camp with Total Goalkeeping, and it was one of the best times I have ever had in soccer camps. Later, I went on the trip around Poland and met with all significant people. I didn't think too much and took the clothes for a not specific amount of time. I didn't know how much time it would take me to think about my next steps. There was only one concern in my head — to go to the United States or not.

At the end of the day, my light backpack and sport bag were too small to prepare me for my big trip around Poland. I wasn't thinking about traveling too much but check out how my trip ended.

Zgorzelec→Wrocław→Kraków→Bielsko-Biała→Kraków→Zamość→Lublin→Gdańsk→Sopot→Gdynia→Karwia→Szczecin→Gniezno→Wilczyn→Świętne→Kruszwica→Toruń→Wrocław→Kraków→Nowy Sącz→HOME.

My dad and I met in Krakow, and then we were together until Szczecin. So, we got some chance to talk, and I told him I wasn't sure about my decision yet. He was so pissed at me, but he didn't force me to decide anything. I knew that he would go regardless of my choice. I left him in Szczecin, and then I joined my family near our great-grandmother's house. We spent some good time with the entire family, even my grandparents were with us. It was super cool to be together. After that, I was dropped at Wroclaw where I stayed at Wiola Brzozka's, one of my closest friends, apartment. We called that apartment "Ziela". My friends and I have a lot of dominant memories from that place. From Wroclaw, I went to Krakow again. I remembered one of my college best friends, Agnieszka Bobrowska, was living just two hours away from there. I texted her I was going to Krakow tomorrow, now look how our conversation went:

Aga: If you are in Krakow, you must come to visit me, it's only two hours away!!!

Me: Tomorrow?

Aga: Yes, tomorrow.

Me: Ok.

If I wanted to go to the United States, I needed to have the best summer ever. If I would stay in Poland, I had to enjoy my time because I didn't want to regret my choice regardless of my next direction. I made over 4 thousand kilometers (more than 2.5 thousand miles) to find just one answer about my future. When I finally got home, I told my family that I still wasn't sure what I wanted to do. However, I really enjoyed my trip, so I looked at Miami's picture on Google. In addition, my family was telling me that I wouldn't be able to find the better time to make the trip — I agreed with them, and had the same point of view. As you could see, I didn't mention soccer at all — it wasn't the key of my choice; the key was a big adventure, and adventuring has become my new hobby. I chose to experience living in the United States and then writing about it. Here we go.

THIRTEEN

BIG SURPRISE

All decisions have consequences, just be aware of it; however, to see the bigger picture, people have to invest their attention to the choice they just made and start living in the present time. Otherwise, they will waste their time and think only about the negative effects of their choice. With that being said, people cannot move forward and leave the experiences behind until they stop thinking only about darkness. Waking up every day with a beautiful view might not be enough to kill that mood. Trust me, I was there, and I couldn't forget about my choice — I couldn't accept the fact that I came to the United States. From the beginning, I thought people shouldn't change the place where they feel comfortable for a sizable question mark, meaning adventure. However, sometimes this adventure might bring much more than just a comfort zone — it might advance into the sense of living — and that's the best feeling I have ever had. Find it sooner than later!

As soon as I decided to go to the United States, I got a lot of advice, especially about making some research before I would move into the new place — Florida. Let me be honest with you, I really got a lot from reading articles and blogs, but I can't say that any of those helped me with facing a different culture. If you go for a vacation, the analysis about temporary living place is necessary — only you know what adventure you are looking for. However, changing the place of living for minimum one year without knowing what exactly you want to do there might complicate everything. As for me, I was going there only to get the experience of living in a unique country. I went to the United States with the purpose to find and understand my adventure. If I knew all the details before I came to the new country, I would never get into that plane to Miami.

Even though I put a lot of effort on the field, I didn't want to be disappointed again. After sending emails to American coaches from Poland, I got no answers. I didn't have many hopes of getting into a college and kicking the ball for their team. I told myself that if there were some benefits for me from soccer, then I would go for it. However, if nothing came up, I wouldn't lose my mood — how could I lose it if I was living in Miami? I just didn't know that the fact of me being alone in the unfamiliar country without knowing the language would make it so complicated.

My dad and I landed in the USA at the end of September 2017. We came by the first plane after the hurricane, so the first days were awful. Everything was dirty and a lot of palms were just lying on the street. If some houses had a fence before, now this fence became their new garden. The views were terrible, and the ocean was very dirty. We couldn't choose a better time to see the beauty of Florida.

Meeting a new culture has always been an excellent experience for me. Every time my dad and I used to walk to a different store, especially when we wanted to meet a new neighbor. We asked our landlord where the closest store was, and he told us the direction with mentioning that the store was a few minutes away. However, the old man didn't mention that we were supposed to go there by car. We didn't know that Americans were telling the distance from the car's perspective. When my dad and I heard that the store was 15 minutes away, we were happy to go for a walk. However, after about an hour, we got pissed because we couldn't see any store. Those minor details which complicated my life were with me for a long time — I was hoping for some adventures in the new place, but not for studying every detail.

I didn't face big problems with the jet lag, so I started

to work immediately. I was trying to get some help with finding a college; however, my contacts weren't able to help me at all, so I was all by myself. I came to the new country without knowing if I had time to present my skills. One day I found a website which showed me all the universities with men's soccer programs. Before I sent my email to the coaches, I checked my message a few times, prepared my introduction, and attached my highlights and resume to the email. I had some days when I could spend the entire day sending hundreds of emails to coaches from different universities. My dad was super mad at me because he hoped that I could find some job shortly; luckily for me, he knew that getting answers from coaches was the first step for me to move on.

Each university in the United States received my email a few times. Literally, every soccer program at NCAA D1, D2, NAIA, and NJCAA level received my highlights a couple of times. I had my own tactic of sending those emails. Every day I was sending emails to Florida because I was interested in that state the most since I was already in Miami. After that, I was sending emails to all the schools from other states, another day = another state. It took me a few weeks before all schools received my email, but the result was the same. Even though I invested my time to approach hundreds of coaches, I didn't get plenty of emails back. Just a couple of coaches texted me back, but most of them were sending the message automatically — I ignored this message. Furthermore, when some coaches texted me back, they asked me about my budget, my college credits, and all other stuff which I didn't know about. All I wanted to do was to get to the official tryouts and show them what I could do on the field. After that, my dad would talk with the coaches because I didn't speak English at all. However, I didn't get a lot of chances, and with each day I got more frustrated about not seeing any ways of playing.

I didn't know that I came in the middle of the soccer season, so most coaches were focused only on the games rather than the recruiting process. My Gmail was silent until I got one answer from NJCAA school, Broward College. The head coach, Munga Eketebi, texted me that he was interested after seeing my videos. At the same time, he offered to meet and talk. Coach Eketebi invited my dad and me to watch their conference game against ASA College Miami. I was extremely happy that finally my main goal in the USA could come true. After my dad and I arrived, we noticed that the stadium looked nice, but the major field was horrible. In addition, my possible future team, Broward College, lost that game 3:1, so my feelings were very mixed. The level of the game wasn't bad, but I would count on something better than that. After the game, my dad and I went to meet with coach Munga. He liked us immediately prior to his experience with players from Polish National team plenty of years ago. When the coach was asking me about some magnificent players from Polish history, I was just pretending that I knew most of them; however, I hardly knew a couple of dominant players from that time. Coach Munga knew almost everyone. Our first conversation went great, and even if I didn't speak English that much, I understood that he would like to see me on the practice before we would talk further about my next steps.

Within the first two weeks in the new country, I was invited for tryouts in Broward College. I had to take care of the physical exam, and then I could attend the practice. From the beginning, I always took my dad with me, so he could talk with coaches after the training. I tried to make some friends, but it was impossible because I couldn't understand anything; I felt terrible about it. I joined the team after they lost an important game in the conference. Goalkeepers and I went to work with the goalkeeper coach — Joe, at that time. He was much older than other coaches, but he had grand experience and character to work. I actually liked his coaching points, but most importantly, he was the first one who told me I belonged to the college level in the USA. It was the initial time after a huge break when I heard very positive words about my goalkeeper skills. After seeing me for a couple of times, coach Munga told me that he would love to see me in spring season with the team. I was surprised because I wanted to practice with them non-stop, but I wasn't allowed to. He said that we would be in touch shortly, and if I needed anything, I just had to let him know.

I have never been patient, so I was still looking for some options. However, I didn't know that I just met one of the most popular players in the USA soccer history. Coach Munga Eketebi achieved literally everything as a player at the college level. Everyone knew Munga except me. I just didn't understand what I was reading about in his bio, sorry, coach! Even though I was still sending a lot of emails, I felt that Broward College could be my only chance to start.

In the meantime, my dad was getting very mad at me because I still didn't find a job. Moreover, from his perspective, I wasn't looking for anything more than soccer. With each day, my knowledge about the U.S. soccer system was getting better. I had to spend enough time before I could understand which way I was supposed to go. At the same time, my dad became my goalkeeper coach, I showed him everything, and he helped me with each drill on the field. To be honest, we were doing a wonderful job with preparing me for the next tryouts — I could definitely make a wonderful impression. With that being said, we went for other tryouts to Lynn University and Florida Gulf Coast University. They were two major programs; however, I wasn't familiar with them at all. The tryouts in Lynn went positive, and I was invited later for more practices. However, I wasn't offered anything at the Gulf Coast University, but in my opinion, I was one of the best goal-keepers who attended the tryouts. I wasn't scared to tell them I would see them around during the next season.

Finally, I had to get to work because I didn't have more reasons to wait, and my dad's sources were about to finish. He couldn't work much because he was recovering after the surgery, so I had to work full time. I really didn't enjoy that part, and changing from college life into adult life wasn't easy for me. Moreover, I didn't have any friends, so every single time when I had a break or a day off at work, I was spending an entire day on the phone talking with my family and friends from Poland. I was complaining every day, and I didn't see the future in the USA. After a couple of months, I still heard nothing about my scholarship. My English was still not great, but luckily for me, I found the place to work. I got a good job at the hotel, and I was making surprisingly good tips. I liked it from the beginning because I could drive very expensive cars as a valet, but later, it became terribly monotonous work. Even though I was making decent money for a student, I was still alone and mad at myself that I decided to come to the USA. A couple of times, I was a few steps away from packing my stuff and leaving to Poland, but I didn't do it. I promised myself that I would give it a chance for the entire year, so I still had a few months left. I was pessimistic about all the possibilities around, but I just didn't understand them because all my friends were my dad's age, and our points of view were much different. So, I just didn't enjoy my daily life.

At the end of January, I received a few emails from Broward College and Lynn University. Both of the schools invited me for another practice. I came for a couple of "captain" practices when coaches weren't allowed to be on the field. They watched me and told me later that I was doing very well; however, I didn't hear any details about the scholarship yet. A few days later, I returned to Broward College for tryouts, and that time I was supposed to spend the entire spring season with them. I didn't have any problems with that, especially because Lynn didn't reach out to me after the captain practices. We were working three times per week at Broward; in addition, I had a full-time job as a valet at the hotel, but I got a chance to have a flexible schedule. My bosses liked soccer, so I didn't have any problems with making good money and adjusting my schedule as needed — I was so happy about that because I didn't have to fight with my dad.

Broward College didn't have a great season, and actually their last couple of years were bad. During that spring the team was doing very well, and everyone was motivated to work hard. I had to work even more to get my scholarship. I was always working hard on the field and was never late. Coach Munga tricked us a couple of times; for example, one time he was late for a practice, and most players didn't start warming up. Coach came fifteen minutes later and called the full team. He asked people who warmed up to make a step forward, so the entire team made the step; then he read the names of the players who did nothing or even worse, who were late to the practice. They had to run a lot, while everyone who just followed the basic rules of training could enjoy the practice. After playing a few games, I knew that I earned my scholarship, even though I didn't hear any details yet. We won almost every game that spring in 2018, but most importantly we didn't lose any of them. Coach Munga was ready to offer me a scholarship.

Before coach Munga told me that he would be happy to see me in his roster for the upcoming season, I was offered to go for last tryouts to Lynn University. They didn't want to decide before they would see me competing for the spot with their recruits. I didn't have to pay anything for the tryouts, so I went there. I was in a great shape, so coaches and players were impressed by what they saw during the tryouts. At the end, coaches told me they just wanted to make sure that I would be the best choice for them. However, they wanted to offer me only online courses when I didn't speak English at all. I wasn't happy about their offer, but I didn't know that I was talking with one of the best schools from the NCAA D2 level. Most likely, if I heard about this offer again, I wouldn't consider any other options. As a result, I didn't take the offer. I didn't want to study online and pretend to learn English. I had to find a better opportunity, so my last chance was with Broward. Therefore, I wasn't sure if I would like to stay in the USA for the next year.

Overall, I wasn't happy at all at my new home. I had to live with my dad, and we couldn't find a way to not kill each other because both of us were used to live separately. Moreover, I missed my family and friends. My English wasn't getting better after spending over 6 months in the U.S. In Florida many people don't even speak English, Spanish is the first language for plenty of them. I just didn't feel good, yet I was really lost in my mind.

As a prisoner of my own thoughts, I was asked again the same question — do I really want this? I truly couldn't answer for that, I was completely lost because I was working hard to get another chance after my big time injury. However, I had to sacrifice much more than just the value of playing soccer. I had to sacrifice literally everything I had been working on in Poland. I almost got my bachelor's degree there, I missed just one year to graduate. I was well-organized back there, and my

college life was incredible, but I missed just one puzzle
— soccer at the top level. With that being said, I was
very curious about how everything would go for me at
the college level. I made some friends with my teammates, and after some time I could talk with them, so
everything became easier. My friends and I went to Key
West, and after seeing this unbelievable place I knew that
I still had something to prove. I was working seriously
during that year, and for the first time I saw some results
of my work — my scholarship was waiting for me in my
room. I bought some postcards from the Key West which
I haven't sent to my family and friends yet. I wrote the
message for each one of them, but also, I wrote a note
to myself:

Podjąłem decyzję.
W 2020roku spróbuję pierwszą próbę podpisania kontraktu
w MLS. Uda mi się, bo lubię
się tym co robię,
. Do tego czasu chcę napisać
swoją książkę.

Gorszczar.

KEY WEST 14.04.2018r.

"I MADE MY FINAL DECISION. In 2020, I am going to try my best with signing the contract at MLS level. I will make it because I enjoy everything what I am doing. I have found my best mood. In addition, before I sign the contract with MLS, I will be done with my first book. For me, Gorszczar."

People didn't believe that I would make it that far, they didn't think I would get any offers from the universities. At the end of the day, I was seen by one of the best universities in Florida. Even though I got something what I came for, I wasn't sure if I would like to take the offer from coach Munga. I wasn't sure if I was ready to invest everything again. To be honest with you, I didn't have a huge hope of even getting a scholarship offer, but I believed in myself from the beginning of my soccer journey. I couldn't waste that chance. I decided to put everything on the table and make the next two years very special for me and for Broward College. Let's go, Seahawks!

LITTLE NOTE FOR COACH MUNGA:

"Coach, I just wanted to thank you for giving me a chance to play for you. You were the first one who gave me a chance to shine again. I was always doing the same — I was working hard on the field, but with the same attitude out of the field. You saw this from the beginning, and that was something that you liked the most in me. Thank you for offering me much more than just the school and two years of playing soccer; you helped me with getting to know the culture in the USA, and you were the one who gave me a hand to survive in the new country from the beginning. I felt that I made a noble choice of choosing to play for you."

FOURTEEN

THE FIRST SEASON

One of the most important things to understand as an athlete is the purpose of the preseason. Most players which I have been working with and many other athletes believe that preseason is supposed to build your stamina and get you ready for the main season. Unfortunately, it doesn't work that way, and the quicker people understand why they need to get in shape, the higher level will the upcoming season be at. Every single time when people hear about practicing twice a day, they complain about the difficulty and the tempo of the camp. However, each coach lets players know about coming back ready for hard work during the camp; almost everyone does it, I have no doubts about it. Players struggle with following the main instructions, and this reckless approach might cost the entire team everything, including having a poor season. While people are enrolled in a team sport, everybody's help and attitude are needed. You win as a team, and you lose as a team — even if just one player fails.

I have never had a problem with self-motivation; moreover, I was capable to create my own program before the preseason. I always wanted to make a major impression on coaches during that time. Every coach watch players as soon as the trainings start. Furthermore, only 11 players can be on the field at the same time, and for me, as a goalkeeper, only one spot matters. I had to take care of that business from the first day with the team. To prepare for my first season, I went back to Poland because I couldn't stay in the USA any longer without seeing my family. I just had to take a break from that unique culture, and all other responsibilities included. If I stayed in Florida, I wouldn't prepare myself well because my focus would be at my job duties. With that being said, I packed my stuff, and after 10 months of being in a different continent, I finally got back to Wroclaw. I had some time to visit my friends before I got to my family house. I could reset my mind which would allow me later to focus on the season. It was one of the best decisions I have ever made. That summer in Poland was great, I was so happy to spend a lot of time with my family and friends; however, in the meantime, I was mainly focused on self-work. I didn't have any excuses prior to weather or meeting with the closest ones. I was practicing every day, sometimes even twice a day. Whenever it was hot or raining a lot, I could use it to prepare my body for the Florida climate. After spending almost my entire break in Poland, I was ready to get back to my upcoming journey. I thought I was ready for the preseason. I truly did my homework. I was working out because I didn't want to get injured before the season started. I put a lot of effort into that since there was never a season without injuries in my career.

One of the most challengeable climates to do outside sports is in Florida. Even though I was doing a great job in Poland, coaches in Florida showed us that almost nobody met the standard requirements based on our conditioning. I was with those people who could run a couple of laps around the field within 1.15 minutes per lap. The more laps we had to do, the more difficult the task became. However, seeing the players who weren't able to run even one lap showed me and other people that they weren't ready to start the preseason. A couple of them got cut even before our first scrimmage. That's sad, but the reality was brutal; if you weren't ready, you were out of the team. Even if I could face the standard tests, my recovery process was very slow. Every day was the same for me. I was waking up early and eating a small breakfast. After that, we had our first practice. As soon as I got home, I would take some snacks and go to the pool. Later, I had to take a quick nap, eat lunch, and get ready for the next practice. After the second practice, I was that tired that I had a headache which didn't allow me to sleep. My entire body was exhausted, and that caused me problems to fall asleep. As I mentioned before, even if I was well-prepared for the season in Poland, I wasn't adopted to have the same quality down in Miami. The climate in Miami was much different for me, and I didn't have any experience how to be prepared for each practice. The first two weeks were very tough, especially for the goalkeepers. Our goalkeeper coach, Sergio Rapuano at that time, was very passionate about goalkeepers fitness and quick feet. After each practice, I was in pain; however, the results were about to come. I have never been prepared better for the season than after working with coach Sergio.

As soon as all of us received the game schedule from coach Munga, I printed this immediately and I hung it on the wall. My roommate, and my competitor for the starting position, Luke Jones, liked this idea from the beginning. Later in the season, he was the one who consistently made sure that the list was always filled out with the latest games. The target was simple — I wanted to win most of the games and keep the clean sheet minimum 5 times during the season. In addition, I was always trying to predict the score of the game — this way I was always prepared with my own goals for the most important games. I kept my target very simple, so with every day I knew why I was waking up and working as hard as I could. I had only one goal — be ready for the pro level after two years in college. However, first, I had to take care of winning the starting position, and learning English to be able to develop in that environment.

To be honest, the preseason ended quicker that I thought it would. Two weeks of work was really nothing. If I messed something up during that time, I probably wouldn't win my starting position. I was well-prepared to start the biggest season in my life. After playing a few scrimmages, I earned my spot in the fair competition. I was extremely proud that I became the starter since the competition was very tough back then, and I wasn't sure who was supposed to start on the goal.

As soon as I was called first to pick the number on my game jersey, it was clear that I became the first choice for each game. After playing many scrimmages and working out with coach Sergio that summer, I was ready for each challenge. My body and mind found the way to collaborate at the highest level without any problems like minor injuries. Our first game in the season was against Eastern Florida State College, which was one of the best teams in the entire country; they were ranked nationally in the top 10. With that being said, I couldn't wait for our first game; moreover, I couldn't wait to beat them at their stadium in Melbourne. Coaches were telling us how important that game would be, and the reasons why we had to win it. The best way to start the season was to play against the best team in our conference. That was the best opener ever. We could be loud from the beginning.

When we arrived at Melbourne, I saw beautiful facilities, and I couldn't be more excited to start the season. The game was very remarkable to me personally because it was my first really serious game after being injured for the long time — I just had to play my best. I wasn't used to warm up in 10 minutes for one of the most extraordinary games during the season. Coach Munga had his own vision of leading the team, and in his opinion, we didn't need over 15 minutes to get ready for the game. He was the boss, so I had to follow his rules. I was stressed enough before the game (in the positive way), and now, I had to do all my drills and rituals within 10 minutes. That was a quick warm up, and even coach Sergio couldn't believe it; however, he turned the stress situation into the big laugh. I was ready to start the game; however, I didn't get enough time to kick even one long ball during the warm up.

The whistle was blown, and after two years of recovering, I was back on the field again. I proved to everyone, mostly doctors, that I wasn't the one who would quit because of the difficulties' level. I faced that challenge; however, it took me two years before my mind and body was collaborating at the same top level. Could you imagine how motivated I was during that game? That was my ultimate prize after dealing with quitting soccer and returning after to earn some benefits. That game was one of those benefits. I was in the mood to play my best, I just felt it. The field was on another level, wet enough to play a good football. I was presenting very well by dealing with any shots; however, I couldn't kick the ball, I wasn't able to lift it. I just wasn't used to play at that type of field — it was too good for me! Me, the guy who was playing on the field where asphalt was better, got a chance to play in fantastic standards. I didn't have a good day with my passes, but I had one of the best games I have ever had. I saved many 1vs1 situations, I could save every free kick, punched every cross, and dealt with defending the area in front of me. When we scored our first goal in that game, I was extremely happy, but I knew that we still didn't finish it. Furthermore, that was our second attempt on their goal, and we punished them with the biggest price; we were the first one who scored the goal. Later, they were sitting on us literally every minute, but I was in my mood, and they couldn't beat me. Next, they got a penalty kick; I wasn't even stressed, and I was happy that I could face it — I love penalty kicks. I saved that shot, and the guy missed later even the rebound. I was lucky, but I was the hero already. At the end of the game, we were playing just outside our penalty area. I had to be everywhere to save the goal; just one minute left where they went with their last attack. They had an exceptional situation to score, but once again, Gorszczaryk, was on the goal. I saved two or three shots in a row — I couldn't even believe it. We won against the best team in our conference at their home field, and I was the key man who helped with achieving that success. After the game everyone was thrilled, and when we shook hands with our coaches, coach Munga told me that when he saw me saving the penalty, he knew that today I was capable of saving every shot made on my goal. That's how we started our season. Another game on the list where I could write 1:0 for Broward College. Now my wall was looking way better.

Even though we achieved something great, I didn't understand the value of it until the athletic director came to us, and told us how proud he was when he heard about the score. He wasn't able to come to that game for the first time since he was working for Broward, and he regretted it so much. I wasn't the happiest man yet because I knew it was a long way before our main success would come. Coaches congratulated us on the first practice after the game, but they reminded us what our goal was, and explained that now we were the primary aim in that conference. We made an enormous sound after that game, and now everyone wanted to show us that this was a mistake. I was ready to prove that I deserved to succeed that season.

A few days later, we were about to play the second big team in the United States, Daytona State College. Based on what I heard, Daytona and Eastern were the major teams who were competing for being the winner of the conference. So, within one week we could face the biggest competitors for the championship. I was highly optimistic about the next game, and I hoped to present myself well like on the first game. This time we didn't have to be stressed about having only 10 minutes to be warmed up. After that game, I understood that our coach just didn't need more time for us to be ready for the game. Even if we played at home, we were the second team on the field before the game started. I wasn't stressed because I knew that I was prepared for that battle. The game started very effectively for us, and we scored first again. However, they tied before the first half ended. I made a couple of big saves and was holding my team with a good score. I knew that we couldn't lose that game; it was our time to shine. I was nervous about the final score because Daytona seemed like they just warmed up, so I knew the second half would be very tough. They were on our half all the time, so I had plenty of job to do. I stopped every shot in the second half and the game ended 1:1. In my mind, I was proud that we tied it and got one point; therefore, the funniest thing for me was when I saw the people who didn't shake the hands after the game. I asked my friend what was going on, and he told me that we were about to play overtime. I thought he was joking, but then he added that we had to play a golden goal. I couldn't believe my ears, I thought the golden goal was only available in FIFA 20 (video game). Moreover, one of our players got the red card during the second half, so that's also why I was so happy about the result, and I could deal with sharing one point in our conference. Rather than having one point, we were about to play another 30 minutes against the team which was up by one player and who was presenting way better in the offense. I knew it would be tough for us to survive, but I hoped to get a good score at the end. The golden goal system was crazy, but, in our favor, we were the first team who scored the goal, and with one player down, we won the game and got the entire three points. We were a solid leader in our conference for now; moreover, we jumped to be nationally ranked. It was amazing, and I couldn't wait for more.

In the meantime, I was studying hard to learn English. I knew that I had to put a lot of effort to make it happen. To be honest with you, I didn't believe that one day I could finally be fluent, but I had to trust the system. I took my classes and was actually doing everything what I was told to do. It was fun and way easier than in Poland, so I could shine in school with earning the 4.0 GPA in my first term in the USA. Also, during my first term in the foreign country, I met Rita Pleskevich, my girlfriend, and I filled my entire free time with spending time with her. I truly wanted to experience the best time ever in America, so I wanted to use all the benefits offered by Florida, but I didn't want to do this alone. Luckily for me, I met her, and she never said no to me. On our first date I took Rita on the beach, she wasn't scared to go with me even if it was around 10 pm... After we met, we spent plenty of time together between our practices and classes. I couldn't be happier than that, I was living my best life; finally, I could play soccer again, I was living in amazing place, and I found the best fit for me. Rita gave me a lot of inspiration to work harder than ever. She was the one who was attending and watching my games regularly, and I was super happy about that. So, for the first time, I saw that somebody was really involved in my life. With every day we had together, we found more and more things to do, and we were never bored or tired of getting back home very late when we had to wake up very early for the next day's practices (Rita even had her practice at 6 am, but I could sleep way longer). I just couldn't describe my dreams better, that was much more than I have ever dreamed for. Thank you, Rita, for making every day very special for me! Now, I was ready for every game in the season.

Our season was going great, and after the first two games, we were the kings of our division. We defeated two of the best teams in our conference. Our third game was against Daytona again, but this time we had to travel really far. Of course, we had some troubles with our bus, so we got late to the game. Actually, we were supposed to play a few minutes after we arrived. Rita quickly wished me good luck, and then I changed and ran to the field to warm up. We had only a couple of minutes; it became normal later, but it was a roller-coaster back then. We had to present well if we wanted to go some-where during that season, and we didn't have time to warm up. Moreover, Daytona was transmitting that game live, it was my first game when somebody could watch it on the internet. It was crazy, but I was so motivated to play that game. Our opponents were attacking us all the time, and I came up with the big save at the beginning of the game. A few minutes after, we started the game. I stopped 1vs1 situation, and then I came up with a couple of more great saves during the first half. We tied 0:0, and it was clear that the second half was to survive the game. I came up with a couple of more big time saves, and we finished the regular time with the same score. We had to play over time again. I knew it wouldn't be that easy and lucky like the first time was. We were defending well, and it was another big game where nobody could score on us. We had a couple of really good chances to finish the game; however, we were very lucky that the game was over after the overtime with the 0:0 score. Our team played as a unit, and we were able to protect our goal well. Commentators were impressed by how my team and I presented, and I was on the primary screen after the game. I was so happy with how I did during the game, but later, I was even happier when Rita texted me how great I was. I was surprised that she found the game because I didn't even know that they would transmit it, but I couldn't be happier to hear that somebody important to me watched my team big success. I was so proud of our team because it was a huge challenge for us to keep it up with the great scores. So, after playing the first three games we had 7 points, and we were on the first place in our division. Nobody was even close to us that time. We were about to face the Eastern State College at home. It was the most important game in our conference; in addition, we knew that if we beat them the second time, we would be very close to be champions after playing just four games in the conference. The tremendous event was coming to Broward, and that was the best schedule we could ever ask for — we could face the best teams in our division first, and then play against ASA College Miami without that tremendous pressure on us.

The fourth game in the conference was about to start, and we knew that Eastern would have to play like their season was about to end. From the beginning the game wasn't easy, but we were extremely motivated to do our best on the field. The first half was very tough for us, and we had to defend our goal most of the time. We did it very well, and I got a chance to be warmed up. I had a lot of things going on during the first half, but I dealt with all of them. We knew that they would attack us all the time, so we could only counter them. We had to do this once, but with everything we had. The second half started with the same scenario, they were on us, all we could do was just to kick the ball out from the field. However, there was one time when we got a very good chance to make a perfect counterattack. Could you believe that we were the team defending the goal all the time, but with two shots on the goal we would be one goal up? We scored, and we were heading to win that game. I was so motivated to keep my clean sheet against Eastern again. The game ended with a couple of great saves for me, and everyone celebrated, like it was the ultimate game of the season. It was great to beat this team again, and the athletic director was the first one who talked with me after the game and told me he didn't know how I did it, but the saves were just outstanding. Moreover, I knew that Rita was with her friends at that game, so I was happy that I played very well as my team did. Also, I had another visitor during that game — my dad surprised me by coming down to the game. He changed my plans a bit because I was about to spend time with Rita, but I couldn't say that I wasn't happy to see him. My dad and I had a good time together, but I couldn't let him borrow my car because I already had plans with Rita. Sorry, dad! Everyone was so cheerful after that game; we knew that we were heading to make that year very special for Broward and for us.

After that game, we knew that we were about to be champions in our conference of 2018/2019 season. Our next game was against ASA College Miami, and we tied the game 1:1. However, I didn't play that game, and other starters got some rest too. Our coach wanted us to be fresh before the most important game of the season — playoffs final! The last game in our conference was against ASA College Miami again, but this time we played at home. We were motivated to play that game, but I felt that most players were thinking only about the next game — the biggest final for us. Luckily for us, we scored four goals against ASA and lost only one. I was so upset about my teammates' attitude for that game. But overall, I was proud of my team since we could keep the clean sheet 3 times out of 6 games. I was ready to play the biggest game in the season. Seahawks, let's get this done!

The last game in our Region was about to come. We

were honored to play at our stadium where all our friends and directors could come and support the Seahawks. All athletes were required to attend that game; it was the first time when our stands were full. I was so excited about that game; I literally couldn't sleep a day before. I knew that this would be the true battle. This time our team got some time to prepare during the warm up, so I wasn't scared about my goal kicks again. When the game started, the Eastern were on us all the time since we won two games against them in the conference. We just had to play our game, and we did this successfully during the first 20 minutes. However, a few minutes later, we made a very simple mistake, and the referee didn't call the foul, which was obviously there. The play wasn't stopped, so all we had to do was a tactical foul, but we didn't do it. They made a perfect counterattack, and one player had a 1vs1 situation with me. I was so close to stop that shot, but unfortunately, I didn't reach that ball. We were down by one goal for the first time after playing big time conference games. I was scared because we had to get back to the game. I thought Eastern wouldn't step back, but as soon as they scored the first goal, they parked the bus in their penalty area. We didn't have enough tools to punish them back then. We were working as a unit without having any special talent, but collaboration was the key to success. Most of the time during the season we were doing very effectively on our defensive part; however, that one play ruined our season, and we weren't able to score the goal in the final. Even though we won twice against them, we lost the most important game in the season. We lost the regional final in Florida. Our season ended just like that.

FIFTEEN

THE SYSTEM

U nderstanding the system is the key to success at any stage in life. Without knowing the basic rules, you might be lost like I was during the first season — I didn't know that we had to play overtime when we tied the game; moreover, I didn't know about the golden goal rule. Most of the time my English wasn't good enough to hear all those details, but I was lucky enough to learn everything during my first season. Sometimes you might have the best season in your life, and win all the conference games, like we did, but at the end of the day, only the true team will get through, and win this one important game of the season — the final game in the playoffs. In addition, the United States soccer system at the college level is not simply about how good you are on the field, but, most importantly, what kind of person you are, and what grades you have. I didn't have any problems to adjust to that system because I was so motivated to master English. I didn't want to be the guy who didn't understand the coach, and missed the great opportunity to play pro because of that. That system has matched with me immediately.

The soccer season was very short, we started at the beginning of August and ended in October. Even though it was a short season, we had plenty of games to play. Sometimes we had two or even three games per week — ranking and conference games. Our coaches told us from the beginning, that year was supposed to be a brilliant opportunity for us to shine since the National Tournament was hosted in Daytona. With that being said, all the best teams in the country would come down to play in Florida. In the climate which only players from there were used to perform. After we lost our last game, coaches told us that we would regret that game for a long time because Eastern would achieve something special. That was true, they went to the semi-final of the National Tournament. Just to remind you, we won them twice during the season. So, that could show us where we were meant to be. However, the system was brutal, and being the champion of the conference wasn't enough to be promoted to the Nationals. I still regret that one game...

After playing my first prime season, I understood way more about playing soccer in America. However, I couldn't believe that after a few months of hard work all players were free to do whatever they wanted to. I had some free of practices time until the beginning of February. I just enrolled to take spring classes, so I was supposed to start them at the beginning of January. I knew it before, so I bought the ticket to Poland last December, and I was partly sad about it because my second half was staying in Florida. When we finished our season, Rita's games were about to start, so she didn't have too much free time. She had only less than one week off during the Christmas break. That was my first time when I really didn't want to go home after being in the U.S. I didn't need any time off; I started to enjoy the system in the USA. Moreover, I had plenty of basketball games to watch.

I went to Poland for about a month, and I counted the days to get finally back to the sunny place. I had a pleasant time, but I understood that I was happy enough at my current home — Florida. That time was necessary to understand that I could be focused on building my future in the America. After spending the Christmas break with my family and friends, I finally took a plane to Miami. Welcome back!

Spring was much easier than fall season. I couldn't

really understand why the coaches were so easy on us, but during spring we didn't play for anything important. The coaches were looking for some changes in the team, so many players were on the tryouts. I earned my spot, so I wasn't worried about the next season. Moreover, after each season we always had individual meetings with coaches.

After the fall season, coach Munga told me that he was extremely happy with what he saw, but he also added that if I wanted to make a huge step forward in my career, I had to gain extra pounds and work on my passing — especially goal kicks. I took this to my heart because I wanted to make the next season very memorable for me and my team. After spring, the meeting was very similar, and coaches were telling me how proud they were because I adjusted to the system quickly. Overall, I had great grades at Broward College, and I made the FCSAA All-Academic Team in Men's Soccer 2018-2019. To be honest with you, I did nothing exceptional. I just followed the basic principles like I constantly did in Poland, but the system here gave me a lot of benefits. I was proud that finally I knew the system way better.

Everything was going great until I understood the NCAA rules. They were very strict, and I wasn't sure if I would be eligible to play at the D1 level. I was super sad about that because I thought Broward College was just the first start in the U.S. system for me. However, I had to make sure that I would graduate from Broward within two years. Most of the time, you must finish your AA-degree after playing in the Junior College to play at D1 level. Moreover, you have only five years to play at D1 level, and this time starts after you graduate from high school. For example, I graduated high school in 2015, so my 5-year clock would end in 2020. My eligibility to play was under a big question mark.

There are few divisions at the collegiate stage in the United States. The highest and the best division to play is D1. They have most of the money, so, most of the time, the facilities are amazing at this level. Also, D1 has the biggest schools, so most of them are public ones where you might qualify for in-state tuition. The next elite division to play is D2, and the rules are different. Instead of a 5-year clock, they have 10 semesters to play. So, if you haven't decided where you want to study after graduating high school, you have some time to think about what you would like to do; however, you cannot play pro prior to the NCAA regulations. In addition, D2 schools are usually private, and they cost a lot of money (most of the time 40k+ per year). So, if you don't have a great academic standard, then it might be a problem for you. Furthermore, the United States offers a less competitive level, D3. At this level you can only get academic scholarship, but those schools don't have any athletic money (the school costs is similar to D2 level). Next, students might go to play at NAIA level where there is no age limit. For example, the NCAA limit is 26 years. However, even these schools are private most of the time, and fees are high as well. That's how the major system for athletes look in the USA. Please notice that everything I mentioned about money is based on soccer; in basketball or any other sports, there are different rules and scholarships.

It was clear for me that I wanted to play at D1 level since I knew that I belonged to the best ones. However, I didn't have any other choice than to stay in Broward for the next year. My girlfriend was moving to the University of Washington, and I was so happy for her since she deserved a chance to play against the best ones in the PAC-12 conference. I had some options to choose from, but after talking with coach Munga, I knew that I hadn't finished my business in Broward yet. He didn't even have to convince me to stay. After spending plenty of time with him on the phone, I believed that he would take care of me as best as he could. I didn't see the reasons to leave somewhere where I had to pay for my living and education; moreover, I didn't know how long the process of the NCAA eligibility center would take to allow me to play. Even though Rita was moving to the farthest place possible, I believed that I could join her for the next year. We both agreed — it was a significant chance for her to develop since her school was one of the best; based on academics and conferences. It was a huge motivation for me to get to the similar level as Rita already was. During my second season, I just wanted to take care of the business. Let's go, Broward.

SIXTEEN

THE SECOND SEASON

As I already told you, athletes are responsible to come for the preseason well-prepared. However, I also knew that vacation time was necessary for me after hard work during my first year at Broward. Rita and I went to Russia, and we spent plenty of time at her home in Moscow, and her summer house where I met her family. Also, we went together to Saint Petersburg. We had almost a month in Russia together, and after that I spent some time with my family in London. In the meantime, we were working with Rita to be in shape for the next season. Even though I was the one who was lazy, she always kicked me to do the practice. The summer was glorious, and from London I came back to Miami. That time I was preparing myself for the upcoming season in Florida since I didn't want to have the same pain and headaches like during my first preseason. I had to be prepared as best as I could because I was named to be the captain of the team. My best friend from Broward, John Davalos, was named the captain as well, so we had to lead the team during our last season at Broward.

I was working plenty of times alone, when I was kicking the ball to correct my goal kicks, and running a lot to be prepared on my conditioning drills with coach Sergio. He would want to kill me again during the preseason, but I couldn't wait for it. I knew my goals; I had two goals — get to the Nationals, and transfer to one of the schools in Washington, which means to one of the best schools in the USA. With that motivation, I came back to finish my last season in Broward. I had to prove myself and other coaches that I could make it to the next level. Nobody had to tell me something twice. I often called our assistant coach, Nelson Valenzuela, if he could work with me on my passing. He didn't have to even think about it; he always said: "See you tomorrow." After that one call, we were working together extra for the entire season.

Before the season started, John and I got together with coach Munga and Nelson to talk about the upcoming fall. Coach Munga was extremely excited about the approaching season, and coach Nelson told us he never saw Munga that happy before. With that being said, I was so proud that I could be a part of his team; moreover, I was responsible to be on the line between the coaches and players — I was happy about that challenge.

When the preseason started, I knew that the team had a great potential to go further than during the last season. We had plenty of skillful individual players, but the biggest challenge was to create one unit to work together as a team. The same way as during the first preseason, a lot of players came in terrible shape, and some of them were cut within the next few days. Coaches weren't easy on us at all, and we had to run a lot of laps again within 1.15 minutes per lap. However, that time I was well prepared for the training; I had a hat and enough electrolytes in my cooler. Gatorade, water, carbohydrates, and protein shakes were always with me. Even coach Sergio wasn't able to kill me during that time, and I knew that he was trying to do it so badly.

I didn't have to fight for the starting position that much during my second season since my competitors were just messing everything up on the way. After playing one scrimmage against Lynn University, coach Sergio called me to say I wasn't allowed to be injured at all. I was supposed to play all important games, and I loved that challenge. Before, I was always struggling with slight injuries, but as soon as I came to Florida, I could finish my first season almost without any breaks; I literally didn't skip any of the practices because of the minor fractures like pulled muscles. So, I knew that I could take care of that season as well.

One of the first games of our preseason showed us that our team was based more on individual skills rather than on group collaboration. That was the problem which John and I had to solve quickly. What is more, the team was divided into small groups based on the culture. Brazilians were spending time collectively, Spanish people were separated as well, and the freshmen were in their group. So, as captains, we were trying to put everything together by creating the certain rules before the preseason even started. Everyone agreed to the team rules; however, when it was time to work, most of them weren't willing to follow them to become a better unit. They just wanted to be outstanding individual players.

That year, I kept only mine season's goals on the wall. I knew what I was working for, so I didn't have to find some extra motivation to push myself off the limits. Couple of times per week, I was working with coach Nelson and John just to correct my footwork. If Nelson wasn't able to make it that day, I was doing extra practice either alone or with John. I realized I had to correct that fragment of my game. The preseason went quickly, and I was ready for the games. I made sure that all players were on the same boat with us, and I explained to them all the rules prior to my experience. That year everyone was familiar with the rules and the system.

For me it was a little tough, and I had some bad moments because Rita wasn't with me regularly. She was 6 hours away by plane, but, at the same time, I had more time to work on my skills to become a better goalkeeper. So, we got through this, and coaches helped me with facing those difficulties as well; especially coach Sergio and Munga. They talked with me a lot, and they taught me how to split the personal life and soccer life, which was essential for me if I wanted to make it to the next level. I was so glad that I had some mentors to listen and follow on my coaching board. Coach Munga became one of them. He was always there for me, and he was the one who told me how significant that season was for me. We were talking plenty of times between the practices about the team goals and my future. I was ready to go.

That year I knew that I couldn't make the same mistakes with my passing, and I was very confident with it after working with coach Nelson. In addition, coach Sergio was preparing me very well for each game. We were supposed to have 14 regular games including 6 conference games; however, the first three games got cancelled because of the hurricane time in Florida. Later, we had a great season opener against Georgia Military College because we won that game 2:1; I had a few top saves and one which saved the game. Most importantly, that team beat us 5:1 last year. So, we realized we were meant to be the important team during that season.

Our schedule for the season 2019/2020 differed from the one from last year. The first conference game was against Daytona State College (away game), then ASA College Miami (home), Daytona (home), Eastern (home), ASA (home again), Eastern (away). As you see, we had to face Eastern only at the end, but I would rather play against them at the beginning like last year. However, we couldn't change anything, and we also knew that now Eastern and Daytona wanted to destroy us. First, we played in Daytona where the game was streamed, so that time my family and friends knew about it. I was so glad to play that game since I knew the level would be high. Even commentators remembered me from the first fall, so it was very fun to play over there again. The game was tough from the beginning, and we had a problem getting on their half. I stopped a couple of grand plays, made good passes, and defended the area in front of the goal very carefully. The first half ended 0:0, but both of the teams had some chances to score. However, the better opportunities were on Daytona's side. During the break between the halves, I talked with the team just before we got back on the field. I told them that we weren't leaving that place without getting three points. The second half was very exciting, and we played way better. Daytona was completely lost, and we had a lot of significant opportunities to punish them. Finally, our team scored the first goal in the season after 70 minutes of the game. Everyone was so happy about it because we were going to our destination. Furthermore, two minutes later, I got the ball, sent it behind the defenders, and created a 1vs1 situation for my teammate who scored the second goal in the opener. We were winning 2:0, and we had the game under control. However, at the end of the game, we made a simple mistake, and we lost the ball easily. It reminded me of our last game in the previous season when nobody could make a tactical foul far away from our goal. Finally, my defender made a foul, but he created a great chance for them to cross the ball. They got a free kick, and they sent a very good ball on the second post. I did my best since I played very effectively outside the goal, so I committed to catch it; however, I got smashed from behind, and I dropped the ball. Then, there was a rebound, and we lost the first goal in the season. Till today my dad and I believe that there was a foul, and the referee just didn't want to call it, but I always had to argue about that play with coach Nelson. He was tough for me, but that was the point. No matter how hard I could be hit, I couldn't drop this ball in front of me, I was supposed to punch it outside the box. After that one "mistake", coach Nelson added extra drills with crosses to our routine, so I wouldn't drop the ball again in that season; I didn't make this mistake again. The game ended 2:1, and overall, I knew that my team and I had a fantastic game. After the game, I was so overjoyed to hear and read all the messages on my phone — from my grandmother Dorota, my girlfriend Rita, and my dad Sebastian. All of them were very proud. In addition, I got even a couple of interests after that game — it was just the beginning of the great season.

Later we had to face ASA, and I knew it would be very important to win that game. Everyone was so confident before the game started, but sometimes disregarding opponents costs you a lot. ASA created some opportunities to score, but I saved everything I had to, and a few minutes later we scored the first goal. We controlled the game, but we did so many simple mistakes, and rather than winning 8:0, we won only 3:0 — coaches weren't happy at all; I wasn't either because we played very selfish. The next conference game was a rematch with Daytona, but this time we played at home. I knew that many people were coming to watch our games since the recruiting process was going on all the time. I had to play perfect games against talented teams, and Daytona was one of them. We talked a lot before the game and set the goals — we knew that the game was crucial in our conference. The first half was quick, and both teams created some scoring opportunities. I did very well on the goal and made one great save after the corner kick. Before the first half ended, we made a perfect play and scored the first goal of the game. During the break our coaches, especially Nelson, told us that whoever scored the second goal would win the game. He used to say it all the time, and almost always he was right. Our team defended very successfully, and after about 10 minutes of second half we added the second goal. All of us knew, we were good, but a few minutes later one player got a red card for a foul. Broward was up by one man; we couldn't lose that game. However, even if they were playing with one man down, they created too many chances to score on us. Moreover, we lost our focus and rather than punishing them by scoring two more goals, we were forced to protect our goal. I was so pissed about it because goals matter in our conference as well. As a result, our team played smoothly, and we kept the clean sheet. We won 2:0, and I saved 6 shots during that game — a couple of them were crucial saves. I was proud of how I played and how our team presented against the top team. As a result, we had the same amount of points with Eastern, but the goal difference was on our side, so we were the leaders again.

The enormous game was coming, and we were about to face Eastern at home. We had to be absolutely focused on winning that game because it would help us win the conference again. Coach Sergio and I already knew that we would never get over 15 minutes to warm up with coach Munga, so we had our own strategy with the drills before the game. I was ready to play the huge game at home. However, we started terribly because we were very stressed on the field as a team. As a result, we lost the first goal within the first 5 minutes. I saw that everyone was extremely disappointed, especially the players from the last year who remembered our last game against Eastern when we weren't able to get back to the game. However, during that game, Eastern wasn't planning to park the bus again, and we knew that this would be an open battle. I did a couple of great saves, so I was holding my team with the same score. Once again, we had plenty of opportunities, but individuals were more important than the entire team, and the first half ended on our lost, 0:1. Coaches were so mad because we had enough chances to score a goal, and we could finish that game during the first half. However, sometimes the ball didn't want to pass the goal line. The second half started, and we played way better — we were forcing them to make some mistakes. We were so determined to score and win that game. I knew I had to play perfect on the goal, there wasn't a time to lose a second goal, so I defended everything I had to. To be honest with you, I hoped that we could score, but I wasn't sure if we had enough tools to make it happen. Finally, from nowhere, our forward made a bicycle kick, and somehow the ball passed the goalie. I couldn't believe that we got back on Eastern! After we scored, we couldn't let them score on us again — in that case, we just wouldn't be able to come back. The game was very close, and we had other opportunities, but we weren't able to finish it in the regular time. We had to play overtime where both teams could win. Remember — whoever scored would win the game. We formed a couple of great counters, but we couldn't score again. We were so unlucky! Despite that, I stopped a couple of dangerous shots during the overtime. The game ended 1:1, and we shared one point with Eastern. I made plenty of saves during that game; they made about 18-20 shots and I allowed only one goal in. Don't get me wrong, I wasn't happy about my game either — for me, one goal was too many, and without that we would win the game.

Coaches weren't happy because they knew how important that game was for us. If we won that game, the pressure during the next games would be on Eastern. Maybe we preferred to check ourselves and see how we would deal with it though. Our next conference game was against ASA. That season, we didn't have to play at their stadium since coaches agreed that our field had much better quality. I just asked my team for one thing — to play the game as a one unit and to work for the team. As a result, ASA wasn't able to touch us at all, and we finished by winning 5:0 at home.

We were way better than Eastern based on how many goals we scored that season — we reached 13 goals before our last game in the conference where Eastern got only 8. All we had to do during that last game was to not lose that game. Then we would celebrate being the champions twice in a row. We were very motivated for our last game, mistakes weren't allowed. That time coach Munga gave us even more time to warm up, so players weren't able to complain about time they were given. If we won or tied that game, we would be the champions of our conference, and then the final of the playoffs would be at Broward stadium again.

The game started in the best way for us possible. We scored the first goal within the first 3 minutes of the game. Everyone was celebrating because we knew that it was very hard to score on us. In the meantime, we dropped our heads, and we couldn't defend properly. In the next 3 minutes, we made a few simple mistakes. One player from Eastern made a good dribble and created the scoring opportunity from outside the box. He punished us perfectly; the shot was made with a perfect technique, and I wasn't able to reach that ball. The game was tied within the first 10 minutes. It was unbelievable; we had the perfect scenario on the table, and we weren't capable of taking it home. The first half was very close because nobody wanted to make a second mistake. With that being said, the first half ended 1:1. The second half was supposed to bring us something special, but, overall, we had a good score by drawing that game. With that being said, it was obvious that they would sit on us until they scored. Coach Nelson always says — the second goal wins the game. He was right again, and Eastern didn't have to wait long; the second half started, and they were up by one goal within the first 5 minutes. They were winning 2:1. It was so hard for us to get up after losing the second goal. I never lost over one goal in the conference games as well; moreover, I had never lost the conference game before in my two years at Broward. Unfortunately, I wasn't able to save the entire game, as well as, we weren't able to reach more than two goals; we gave up that game 3:2. This time we had to play the semifinal before we could come back to Eastern for the last game. Our entire season was on the line.

We knew that most likely we would have to play Daytona again at our home, but we weren't scared of them at all. Daytona defeated ASA in the quarterfinal, so the first serious opponent was coming to our place. We were motivated to win that game, and I asked our team to play as one unit again. When we were collaborating with each other, we were playing very well, nobody could hurt us. Our team played very good, and we won our first game in the playoffs 2:1. We could overcome the game with more goals, but, at the same time, we had a possibility of playing overtime with that team again — luckily, I made a valuable save on the line at the last minute of the game. So, we were happy that we won it in the regular time. It was a big win for us because everyone knew how hard it would be to win 3 games in one season against Daytona. After that game, our focus was only on destroying Eastern — we had unfinished business from the last season.

It was a very important game for my team and me. If we lost that game, it could be my last game for Broward College, but I wanted to play as much as I could. Moreover, my girlfriend was coming to watch that game from Seattle. My dad was planning to come as well with his friend, Ziuta. I knew many coaches would come to Melbourne and watch that game as well. My grandparents could watch the game live on YouTube — their support was and still is very meaningful for me. That time we weren't that lucky from the beginning, and we didn't score within the first few minutes. Both teams were playing very secure. Nobody wanted to make a dumb mistake which could cost everything. The first half ended 0:0, and I had one important save already. I felt confident about our shape at that game, but, unfortunately, I got hit during the first half on my muscle — I could barely run. When the muscle got big, I couldn't bend my leg. However, I had to play that game, I couldn't let it go. My goalkeeper coach Sergio saw me, but I said that I was fine. I knew we were going hard on them after the break. I came up with the big save at the beginning of the second half. I saw nothing, but I was set at the right place, so I could make a great reaction save.

Even though we were playing correctly, we weren't the first ones who scored the goal. At the beginning of the second half, we weren't able to kick the ball far away, and it landed just a few yards outside the box where the player from Eastern hit it without the extra touch. I didn't see the ball, but I tried to react quickly. However, it wasn't enough to save that shot. We were down by one goal in the final, so we were very frustrated — we knew that this was supposed to be one goal game again. I hoped that we could get back at them because we had much better individual skills compared to the last year. However, after that goal we failed together as a team. We lost the second goal after the next 3 minutes of the game, and the third one just a few minutes after. To summarize, we lost 3 goals within 10 minutes — it was unbelievable, we just couldn't do anything. The game was already over. In our heads we knew that the game ended after losing the first goal. In the next 15 minutes of the game, we lost the 4th goal, and we just wanted to leave that field. We caught the contact by scoring two goals — first one in the 82nd minute of the game, and the second was in the 84th minute. It gave us some hopes, but we didn't have enough time to punish them and get to the overtime. We lost the second final in a row, but that game was even worse than last year. No goals in the first half, six goals in the second half — today, I still can't understand how it happened. I was disappointed because we had a better team based on the soccer skills, but we weren't a real team — that's what killed us. We were arguing with each other too much, so when it was extremely important to cover each other's back, we would kick each other rather than protect. That cost us the title of the conference champions and the entire season. In addition, Eastern got that year to the finals of Nationals, but they lost it. I wished that we could be the team which went that far, and we could make it happen. As a leader of the team, I wanted to take responsibility for our loss. I talked with coach Nelson after the game, but he told me I did a great job and couldn't blame only myself. He said — you win as a team, and you lose as a team. REMEMBER THAT.

SEVENTEEN

THE CAPTAIN – THE LEADER

The leader is someone who can be responsible for everything and everyone. Moreover, to become a captain you must be mature enough to step forward in front of everybody, and convince them to choose the right way to succeed. The leader is not scared of talking in front of the other people, they know that this is a necessity. The captain is someone who constantly tries to be in front of everybody, and works harder than anybody else to earn the respect from the teammates and coaches. The leader forces their army to do something extra, but is also first on the line to run a punishment or extra lap. The captain is always on the line between the coaches and the players. If somebody from the team messes something up from the organizational side, the captain needs to figure out how to not involve bosses — coaches. The leader has to create the best environment for all teammates; creating their own team goals, organizing team meetings if needed, collecting team money, talking about team rules, explaining all the NJCAA and NCAA rules for new players, and helping each other out to move forward into the next level. If something doesn't work in the team, the coaches would talk to the captains first because they should take care of it. In other words, the captains fail when something isn't organized well for the entire team, and achieve the biggest success when the environment for the players is safe and fair for everybody — everyone would develop as one unit, one team.

The communication in the team:
Coaches

Captains

Players

My friend John and I were named to become captains; we were supposed to take care of the team during our last season. I couldn't wait for that challenge.

It gave me tons of motivation because I realized that I would have to be one of the best in the team based on my shape and game. Basically, I understood that I had to get rid of the simple mistakes during my games, so I worked even harder to correct my passing. I asked coach Nelson and John to work with me on that part. I was expecting a lot from myself and from each player on the team. With that being said, I was very well prepared for the upcoming season; my shape was excellent, but I didn't stop working out on my weaknesses during the season. Nelson was always staying with John and me after the practice to work on kicks and crosses.

Before the season started, John and I organized the meeting with coaches; however, only coach Munga and Nelson could make it that night. Our goal was very simple — we wanted to get permission for our team rules which we created together before our first meeting on the physical day. We talked a lot about the upcoming season, and everyone was excited about our possibilities based on the talents we had in our team. We showed our team rules to coaches and asked if they would agree for those terms. Coach Munga laughed, and told us that we were named the captains, so we had to organize everything like we wanted. It meant coach Munga wouldn't get involved in that process — we could prepare the rules on our own, so we did.

GOALS: WINNING THE NATIONALS

The way to do it — winning our conference (each game), Regionals (each game), and Nationals (each game).

IMPORTANT TEAM RULES

1. No arguments on the practice between the players.

2. Always listen to your teammates.

3. Goalkeeper is the boss on the field (defensive side).

3. Running after losing games — on the same day or the day after.

4. If you are arguing or fighting with somebody, you are out of the practice.

5. Warm up usually will be set on the field, if you need extra time come earlier to the practice.

GENERAL RULES

1. No earrings, chains, bracelets, and flip-flops on the field.

2. No late arrivals.

3. No bottles on the ground.

4. No bibs all over the place.

5. A teammate who is not participating in the practice

because of the injury must help with having the water bottles full.

6. Nobody can miss the practice, if anyone gets hurt, he must show up and support the team or work with the trainer.

7. We are recommending bringing something to eat right after the training, especially during the preseason.

8. The day before every game everyone must help to clean our stadium (no bottles or papers near the players benches)

9. Everyone must pick up all the equipment after the training, nobody can stand next to the bench without helping each other.

10. Stretching after practice, which is run by the captains.

FRESHMEN

1. Pick up all the equipment from Munga's office at least 15 minutes before the practice, and return it after we are done.

2. Do the water before the training, and after training fill it up again for the girls' training.

3. Collaborate with your new teammates, respect goals and rules.

Overall, John and I worked on every detail in preparing our team to avoid any needless troubles during that season. The goal was set, and we wanted everyone to be on the same page. If I could do just one correction to all of that, then I would print rules for everyone, and ask for their signatures. As you could see by the rules, there wasn't anything phenomenal, so we were expecting and looking for the maturity of our team. I wanted to create even better environment than from the previous season, and correct all slight details to make our lives better. John and I were always on time to prepare the warm up sector — we were splitting the duties between us. After the practice we would run the final stretching and summarize something important for the team. Everyone could always say and add anything they needed to. We wanted to be well-organized and mature team who was ready to win everything that fall.

Personally, I believe that everything was well-coordinated, and we didn't have any troubles as the entire team. However, as a leader, I could learn a lot during that season, and one of the most important things I learned was the culture difference. John and I expected that nobody from the team would talk after we finished our first phase of the warm up which was the small monkey game. Later, we were doing dynamic warm up with some mobility exercises at the end — this was the stage when the culture differences were shown. Our team consisted of plenty of international players and couple of local ones. We had players from all around the world — Europe, south America, north America, Africa. The players' age didn't matter, but, after the time, I understood that rather than creating one unit, we were building small groups where players were talking in their native languages. I was always neutral, but I wanted to create a positive atmosphere inside the team. I was always with the players, so I was jumping through each group. What frustrated me the most was that many players just weren't able to adjust to the team goals. Everyone had their own visions which were great. However, at the end of the day, we didn't exist without the team. So, the first thing I learned was about under-standing where everyone came from, only after that I could make some adjustments. The next thing I learned was that not everyone had the same personal goals and reasons why they were on the team. Not everyone sacri-ficed everything to be at that place, and not everyone was willing to sacrifice everything to move forward. However, I believe that if somebody doesn't like the situation at the current place, they can always leave, or change the place to play for someone else with no conse-quences. Some people play soccer just for fun where others play as their life depends on it. With that being said, I wanted to have people on the same boat since I really sacrificed everything for getting the chance to follow my dreams. Even though some rules were too difficult for some players to follow, I think they at least got a preview of how everything might look at the higher level than Broward.

Being the captain was a superb feeling, and I wanted to be involved everywhere I could to help my team succeed. At the end of the day, the team's success equals to every individual player's success, so I was extremely motivated to win first as a team, and then move forward as an individual. I was honored to take the challenge of being the captain of the team; moreover, I could learn from my own mistakes. Those two main things about leading the entire team helped me a lot with understanding the difference between the players, and helped me to see which players deserve and belong to the highest level. I was ready to make some adjustments, especially for our spring season when the rules didn't have to be that strict. Moreover, I wanted to prepare all freshmen to be ready to lead the team for the next season. I truly believe that everyone could see many positive aspects of John and me leading the team, especially from the organizational part. Also, most importantly for me, I wanted to show returning players what I have learned after making some mistakes, so the next generations in Broward would be ready to be the National champions at the NJCAA level. The teams don't win because they consist of talented soccer players; teams win because they are one unit, excellent soccer players, but most importantly, they are all on the same page and want to succeed, so from the mental aspect they are way in front of other teams on the field. Good luck, Broward!

LITTLE NOTE for coaches and players from Broward College:

"First, I would like to start by saying big thanks to coach Munga for giving me a chance to continue my dream. I wasn't certain at all that my passion would bring me that many profits out of the field. Within two years, I graduated from Broward with my AA degree, but most importantly, my English has become very fluent. Coach Munga, thank you for being my mentor and helping me out with understanding what actually matters in life. You were the perfect example for me that hard work always pays off. I would like to pursue working with you in the close future. Once again, I couldn't be happier to say that you were the one who opened the door for me to the USA. Moreover, I wanted to thank coach Nelson who put my skills into the next level and always treated me as a part of his family. I could always count on him, and no matter what, he could count on me. I won't be able to forget our workouts at 6am before the season or our extra time working on my footwork after regular practices. Another great mentor who always could give me plenty of advice which path would be the

best for me — I honestly appreciate all your work for me, coach! In addition, thanks to coach Sergio who brought and forced me to achieve the next GK level. I know that I wasn't always easy, and my charisma could be ignorant sometimes, but I regularly listened to your advice, and even if I didn't agree from the beginning, I understood later that you were right. Thank you for bringing my mind into this special season and for opening me the door to my future. Later, big thanks to coach Joe who was the first one to tell me I was good enough to play for great programs in the America. In addition, I would like to mention here coach Mike and all players from Broward because without them we wouldn't be able to make it that far. I was proud to be a part of the Broward men's soccer team. Also, thank you, John, for being a great captain with me during that season, I think we made a big difference for Broward's organization. I wish all my coaches and teammates all the best in the future, and I hope that everyone learned plenty of things. I know that I wasn't easy on all of you, but overall, I just wanted to move forward and continue my dream like most of you! Good luck!"

EIGHTEEN

WHAT HAPPENS NEXT?

FGCU

"You can go different direction, but you want to go to the same destination." — MG.

P laying for Broward showed me how important it was to follow all the rules. You had to be great, but not only on the field, you had to be able to take care of the business outside soccer. Many athletes fail in one of these main paths, and most of the time it is academic issues. Broward College was simply the first stop for me, I knew that this was only two years of playing when I couldn't even get my bachelor yet. However, I was extremely determined to make another step in my student-athlete career. I didn't lose my routine of sending the emails to unknown coaches since I knew that I had to put a lot of effort to make them like me. Believe me or not, but I didn't receive plenty of calls without emailing on my own. Once again, all the schools from the NCAA D1 and D2 received my email. Moreover, Florida schools got them several times. Even though I played in Florida, I didn't get that many calls as I expected to receive. And that's after playing two great seasons where I made the first team during my first season and the second team in my last season at Broward. Also, I was awarded the FCSAA All-Academic Team in Men's Soccer. I did everything right to move forward, so guess how many full rides I had received.

I was proud of my team, myself, and what we achieved for Broward. We put BC on the soccer map in the USA. Every coach knows that if you can play effectively in Florida, you can present your best everywhere else. The soccer level in the south is one of the best in the U.S. We weren't able to finish our job and go to the Nationals; however, we lost to the team which went all the way to the Nationals, and they were close to win the whole tournament twice — that just shows you the level I played at. With that being said, I had huge hopes about my future in the USA since after my first year, I could already go to the champions' team, Barry University, at that time. I got a chance to play for a team which would defend the championship in the NCAA D2; however, the offer wasn't better than the one I got from coach Munga, so I didn't go there. Within three years in Florida, I got a

few good offers from the top schools in the America —
Lynn University (#2 in the country), Barry University
(the champion in season 2018/2019), Palm Beach
Atlantic (#7 in the country), Nova University, and
University of Tampa. Don't take me wrong, I didn't get a
full ride, almost nobody gets a full ride with athletic
scholarship, but if I had a little more money in my
budget, I would commit to one of these schools. Out of
11 schools at D2 level in Florida, I got some good interests from 5 of them — I could write even more schools,
but I stopped talking to them at the very beginning. It
was because I didn't see the reasons to go there and play
for free if they weren't doing that well like the other
schools. In addition, my remaining eligibility was under
a question mark for everyone, and because of that I lost
plenty of other offers.

Finding the best place for me to play took me a good
couple of years. In Poland, my injuries were happening
regularly because of the weather and temperature, especially when goalkeepers weren't used during the practice
at all while it was snowing or raining. As soon as I got to
Florida, I didn't even have to warm up — I just had to
get to the field and I was already whole wet on the way.
The heat was crazy sometimes, but, at the end of the
day, it was a pleasure to practice in any condition — sun,
rain, and wind; it wasn't a problem at all. I didn't have
almost any breaks during my two years at Broward, so I

knew that I wasn't willing to leave Florida without the impressive deal on the table.

I talked with plenty of coaches, trust me. Sometimes I didn't even remember who I was talking to since I had too many phones on the schedule, and some coaches weren't planning to make the appointment to talk, they just called me. However, to receive all of these calls, I had to send a lot of emails again. I was trying to understand how it was possible that I played so well, and I didn't get enough calls without sending my emails. I can't blame them — those coaches receive like thousand emails daily, so I understood how the recruiting process looked like. I didn't want to go to any tryouts, especially to the ones where I had to pay — no way that I could pay $1, so somebody could watch me play, unless it was tryouts to MLS or USL. With that being said, many coaches from D2 weren't willing to pay for my official visit, so I wasn't interested in their schools anymore — simple as that. I had to visit the school before I would move into my new place.

Before our season ended, I was offered to go for the official visit to Bryant University. It was the only one school from D1 which wasn't scared to help me out. As I understood later, almost everyone treated me by following the standard system — "if you don't have two years now, you won't get them later", but I just needed some help with that. I knew I could get them. The visit went great, and they amazed me with their facilities. Even though it wasn't the warmest place to be at, I could forget about the Florida climate for the next two years. I had a really good offer; moreover, the academic standard of the school would definitely help me in my future. Even though I didn't see the actual contract on the table, Bryant offered me about 30k athletic scholarship money. That was the best offer I have ever gotten from school in the USA. I didn't have to pay a dollar from my pocket, but I had to take a student loan which I was willing to do. There was only one issue before my commitment — Bryant had to hear about my remaining eligibility from the NCAA. Unfortunately, it never happened, and the offer was gone — just like that. Thanks to the whole system!

All we had to know was my remaining eligibility status; moreover, the NCAA didn't even have to confirm that, but they had to let them know that it was possible to give me some years to play. After the time, I understood the coach's situation more, and I was never mad at him because he invested money in some other goalkeepers. I was fine with that, and I was thankful for their work for me with the NCAA. I had to move forward; however, my case wasn't great at all. Coach Munga called me one day and said that he was tired of answering the phone and talking about me every day (he was joking, of course). I was spending plenty of time sending emails to other universities, and my coach knew that. I got some small interests from D1 schools, but as soon as they found out my eligibility situation, they weren't interested in doing some extra work. Only because the NCAA didn't tell me anything back then, I lost a lot of brilliant opportunities to develop on the highest level academically and athletically. They forced me to wait until April 1st when I could request my amateurism status. I thought they would solve everything around that time.

The standard system told me I didn't have remaining years to play at D1 level, but I could play only one year at D2 and NAIA level. I did my research, and I knew that it didn't make sense for me at all. I was ready to quit soccer again, and enroll in public school in Florida to finish my degree. I was trying to find a peace again since I lost almost all my hopes of moving forward. I really invested everything I had; I put everything on the table, but the system was about to trick me again. During my two years at Broward, I had 6 clean sheets in conference games, so one entire season nobody could score on me. Everything was great, and I was so proud, but I knew that I deserved a chance to play at the higher stage. I just wanted to do it, but all the complications have been forcing me to quit again.

I waited for the answer until April, so all my current offers were gone. I thought I would know all my answers within the next few days after my amateurism status was known. I was checking the status every hour, and one day Rita and I found out that I was certified to compete. I called coach Munga to tell him about it, and he was happy since he thought I got two years. I was reaching out to all the coaches I talked to. Everyone told me that they already found a GK for the next season, even Bryant University coach told me they didn't have the same money for me since they had to move forward with getting ready for the next season. I was waiting almost the entire year to hear about my eligibility, and as soon as I got some news about it, all offers were gone. Great.

I was extremely sad about it, but I couldn't quit without giving it one last chance. I told myself that I would send the emails to coaches from Florida one last time. I wasn't interested any longer to play at D2, so I sent emails only to D1 — to Florida International University (FIU), Florida Atlantic University (FAU), Jacksonville University, and Florida Gulf Coast University (FGCU). I sent the emails in the afternoon, and before I was falling asleep, I received the answer from FGCU to set up the phone call on the next day. I couldn't sleep again because I wasn't sure if I would like to go there prior to my previous experience with them. In addition, as soon as I woke up, I got other emails. That time I got the answer from Jacksonville University and the head coach from FGCU, coach Jesse. I set up the calls with them on the same day.

I didn't have time to wait, and I needed to hear some answers about my future. First, I talked with the coach from Jacksonville who told me they had to find out my eligibility status first before they presented me their offer. I was surprised because I thought I got two years to play; we ended our conversation with no specific details. Later in that day, I had phone call with the head coach from FGCU, Jesse Cormier, who told me everything about their program. Since I visited their school before, I knew that he wasn't messing around. Their program has been very solid for a long time, but, most important- ly, the school was known as a great athletic program in the USA. He told me he would love to have me in his team, and as soon as he heard recommendations from plenty of coaches around Florida, he was sure that I was the right choice for him. What surprised me the most, was that coaches who were our conference rivals, were talking highly about me, and that put my name in front of everyone in the recruiting process.

Sometimes you just had to be lucky, I was trying to get in touch with FGCU before, but they didn't need the goalkeeper back then. All the schools that I was interest- ed in Washington and Oregon had the same situation with goalkeepers. Literally, nobody needed a goalkeeper for the next season, I was very sad because of that.

However, unfortunately, the starter from FGCU got injured, so that opened the spot for me in the great program. I was extremely excited about that opportunity, and after talking with the assistant coach, Sheldon Cipriani, I was ready to commit with FGCU. I called the head coach on the same day and told him he found a new goalkeeper for the next season.

Within the next few weeks my application process was completed, and I was accepted to the university. However, one day I received the call from coach Jesse who told me we would have big problems with my remaining eligibility. They offered me their help and decided to fight for my remaining years at D1 level. Everyone agreed for this fight, even the Athletic Director who made the last call with it. I had to get all the documentation, and write a letter for the NCAA, which I did immediately. I was super mad because I thought I was set with the NCAA, but even later, in May, I didn't get any answers. I wasn't patient at all, and obviously I couldn't afford to wait that long — I was exploding inside. After I submitted all the requirements from compliance, a couple of follow-up questions came up, and I needed coach Munga's help. I wrote all other essays in one day, but, most importantly, I needed a letter from my head coach who would write why I deserve the extra year to play at D1 level. To be honest with you, after I read that letter, I was thrilled by everything I have done in Broward. If this was my last season to play soccer, I couldn't be more thankful that I was playing for coach Munga. Here is the letter he wrote:

To Whom It May Concern,

Michal Gorszczaryk is student-athlete from Poland who starred for me at Broward College in the NJCAA Division. It took a lots of patience and luck for his family to emigrate to the United States. He arrived in a new country where he had to overcome language barrier and a new culture. Despite all that, he never lost the focus of getting his education in order to strive in his new environment. He took intensive English classes to assimilate quicker. He had part time jobs to help the family settle. He never lost his passion for soccer and realized that it could be a vehicle to put him through school. As soon as he stepped on campus, I knew I had born leader joining the group. His work ethic and dedication won everybody over. It was just natural that he would be team captain. Michal not only excelled on the field but in the classroom as well. He has consistently toiled over a 3.75 GPA. He has distinguished himself in everything he has done. Some professional teams were interested but he always made it clear that getting a Master is his ultimate objective. These are some trying times for Michal as he waits to hear how much eligibility he will be given. He pretty much put himself through school with his Athletic Scholarship. He is banking on the same thing to obtain his Bachelor. Michal works on a weekly basis with youth organizations as well. He feels that it is important to always give something back. It has been an honor to coach such an outstanding individual.

Sincerely,

Munga Eketebi Head Coach Broward College Men's Soccer

People might invest everything and achieve nothing. People might think they are great, but that greatness doesn't pay off. Sometimes being at the correct place and the correct time is more important than being the best on and off the field. The timing is one of the most influential things to find, but unfortunately, not everyone can find it — people might never find the perfect time that would allow them to become professionals. That's just life, and I was one of the athletes who couldn't find that perfect timing to move forward. I know that I really tried, and everyone around me knew that, but was it going to end without a happy ending?

One of the hardest things for me was to let all my dreams go. Without asking for some help, I got another chance to come back on the field. I used it and proved that every doctor who told me I couldn't play soccer anymore was so wrong. All I wanted was to get my degree, and used one more year to prepare myself for

MLS. I know that I wasn't ready yet to play at the highest level, but the saddest part for me was to be aware of how close I was with belonging to the top. I was asking just for one year to play at D1 because I knew that I could find all my answers after that year. I could make a decision with choosing my future path and answer for that question — DO I REALLY WANT THIS?

TO BE CONTINUED

THE PASSION = THE FUTURE

PRISONER OF HIS OWN THOUGHTS

THE OTHER SIDE

NINETEEN

THE END...

Someday people might be forced to find a unique way to go since plan A didn't work out. Having plan B is one of the most needed requirements for all athletes. The sport journey might end quicker than it was supposed to. Sometimes people might lose everything in one day, just because of the stupid realities in sport — injuries. As I have learned from my experience, without plan B I would struggle everywhere, and I wouldn't know what to do besides school and practices. During my soccer time, I could learn plenty of things besides the skills on the field. I was learning about dealing with life difficulties. One of the most important things I under-stood was how people near you might change your life. Without having great contacts, it could be much harder to move forward to plan B; moreover, I wouldn't know which road to choose without having mentors near me.

I wouldn't be mad at the NCAA if they told me I couldn't play soccer anymore. I could deal with it; I was mad at them because the waiting time has been driving me crazy. Even though I have had a lot of opportunities around, I couldn't make any steps since I had to wait for the answer about my remaining eligibility. All I wanted to know was their ultimate decision. No matter which path I would have to go, I would be more than happy if I could find peace with that choice.

Even though I invested everything I had to offer, I knew that my soccer journey would end shortly. However, I wasn't scared of it, and I already knew which way I would like to go after. Before I came to the United States, I started to coach goalkeepers, and from the beginning I knew that I found my passion — I could be on the field all the time. My biggest motto in life is to do something I like, something I could do for free all the time — I want to have a job which I love. With that being said, I was investing plenty of time besides the school and practice in coaching. I was just getting ready to leave the field as a player and enter the gate as a coach.

Furthermore, I came to the USA to find some bene-fits of playing the game I love, and I found more than I could even ask for. I met the person who literally helped me with everything in the foreign country, and also, who showed me that soccer could be the primary gate for me to move in many directions. Taking the risk of moving to the USA was one of the best decisions I have ever made based on all my opportunities around. Moreover, I have grown up enough to find out which way I would love to go after I finish kicking the ball. For me, it would be the end of the first and long journey, but the beginning of something I wanted to be a part of. All I had to do was to find the answer to the same question — DO I REALLY WANT THIS?

Again?...

TWENTY

...THE BEGINNING

F inding my new hobby was one of the toughest tasks to do in my life. My grandmother, Dorota, gave me one of the best examples of dealing with failures — clearing the mind is necessary at any level and any stage. I was slowly forced to back off from the field, but I couldn't see that all I had to do was to step back as a player. I had to leave the goal, but I could still be a part of soccer. I was about to become a coach.

Before I understood how much I really love soccer, I was extremely disappointed because of the game. I achieved nothing; moreover, I thought that I lost more than I invested in that game. It took me about two years before I got over it, but I could never move forward without finding a new passion in the game. I remember that I had to come to my hometown, Zgorzelec, and visit the military commission. One of my coaches and friends was on that commission board, so I didn't have to be too long in the line to get everything done. While I was asking some questions, he also asked me about my current situation since he didn't hear any updates lately about my soccer career. I told him how I did in Wroclaw and about my surgery. He was the one who suggested me to run one session for goalkeepers from Nysa Zgorzelec, my first club I played at. I said that I could run a session anytime and show some useful tools to young goalkeepers. We set the goalkeeper practice on the next training day.

I had never run a GK session before, but from the beginning I felt that I had a great contact with young keepers. I really enjoyed being the guy who could give some advice on making their skills better. We started to work with each other regularly, so I was coming to my hometown more often. Sooner than later, I got an idea to create the mental program for youth goalkeepers. Do you remember my meeting with coach Jarosław Muracki from TGK? We met in the cafeteria at my university. That day, I told him I would like to come back to the training, but it wasn't our major topic that we talked about. The primary subject was to create the mental program for goalkeepers, and I wanted to be the head of it. Jaro and Artur, the owners of Total Goalkpeeing, didn't have to think long about that idea. They were happy to start this project. We picked the best goal-keepers to work with, and I was meeting with the players on the interviews once per month. I was creating the questions, and coach Jaro was helping me out by improving them. Moreover, they were about to find a new goalkeeper coach for their academy, so guess who was the first guy that they wanted to talk with.

Just like that, I found new passion from the game, but most importantly, Jaro and Artur opened me the gate to become a goalkeeper coach. They picked me to start the internship and taught all their methods and coaching points. I was lucky since I was in their system as a goalkeeper, and even if I didn't like their manners from the beginning, later, I became the biggest fan of it. So, all I had to learn was how to be a coach. Jaro and Artur spent a lot of time with me, and I was proud to learn from the ones who I truly admired.

Before I started the internship, they were familiar with my situation about the chance of going to the USA. They were fine with it, I just had to be involved as much as I could. I didn't fail once, and I really put a lot of effort into work with them. I found the place I wanted to be at. After the entire internship, I was about to coach at their camp. It was my first goalkeeper camp where I was coaching, not playing. It was a brilliant time, and we had a great program to run, we even added the mental training for everyone. I obviously loved everything I had, but unfortunately, I was forced to find the answer if I was going to the USA or not.

I had a couple of talks with Jaro about my future, and I told him I had to find the answer on how far I could go in soccer as a player first. However, I didn't want to lose the chance to work for Total Goalkeeping, and then Jaro told me that I wouldn't lose it since the bag of experience is one of the most important tools for each coach. He told me that whenever I come back, the spot for me would be open. With that being said, I had a rational mind to take a risk and follow the biggest adventure in my life. Welcome to Miami!

TWENTY-ONE

THE RISK

I didn't have any contacts outside Europe, so I wasn't sure if I could continue my coaching and playing careers. However, even with jet lag, I could find out all available coaching courses in Florida. I didn't speak English that well like I thought I could when I was in Poland, so I feared how many things I would understand during my first courses in the U.S. Within the first two months, I already had the goalkeeping courses level 1 & 2 which would allow me to work in south Florida. During the course, I understood a lot of things and got some necessary tools, so I felt ready to work.

First time in my life I was sending my resume to local soccer academies to be hired as a goalkeeper coach. I didn't have to wait long for the answers, and soon, I had scheduled a few phone interviews. One of the major opportunities for me came from Juventus Academy Miami, so I asked the director if we could meet in person and talk about the details. In the next few days we were about to meet, so I prepared the entire program for goalkeepers with different age groups. The interview didn't look like I thought it would, but I got the chance to present my way of running GK sessions. My dad and I had to drive for about an hour to that place where I had my first goalkeeper practice in the USA. Even though my English abilities weren't great, I could run very productive sessions since I was preparing for each one of them before; I knew all the coaching points and how to explain the exercises. I really liked the place and felt that I could stay there much longer, but the director wanted me to work for free at the beginning. He told me he had to see how well I would work with the kids. I was so upset about it, and I told him I couldn't afford it. I wasn't going to get paid at all, which wasn't the most important thing for me back then, but my dad was pissed because he had to waste his time to drop me at their facilities (one hour drive each way). I just lost my first opportunity of doing something I would love to do from the beginning of my U.S. journey. The place was just too far, and I didn't have my own car back then. It was impossible to join them without getting any benefits of that.

Later, I wasn't able to find any other place to coach for a long time, so I had to find a temporary job in the hotel to make some money. When I met coach Munga for the first time, I didn't know who he was in the American soccer industry. Apparently, he was a famous college player, and a magnificent coach at FIU later in his career. Everyone knew him, literally everyone. As soon as coach Munga saw that I was very responsible on the field, he was able to help me out whenever I needed it. One day, my dad, coach and I were talking about my offer for the next year, and somehow, we turned our conversation into a coaching part. I mean, I didn't understand too much of what they were talking about, but I remember that my dad told coach Munga how I was trying to coach at Juventus Academy. When coach Munga heard that I would love to coach, he didn't wait long to make a phone call to his close friend. He called Tom Mulroy, who was the soccer director at Weston Select and AYSO644, but also a great professional soccer player in the USA, and asked him if he needed new goalkeeper coach. Tom said that he always looked for recommended coaches, so I could meet Tom on the next day.

From the beginning, Tom and I made a great relation-ship because he loved Polish people. He told me plenty of stories from his soccer career when he could play with great players from Poland. Because of that, he wanted to see my skills right away after our conversation, so he brought a couple of his goalkeepers, and I could run the session. After that, he told me he would like to have me there in the coaching staff; moreover, he wanted me to coach small kids U6 as well. I wasn't sure if I could make it since my English wasn't that fluent yet; however, I wanted to try. I really liked it, and I wanted to join his team from the beginning, but I wasn't able to modify my schedule in the hotel since I changed it so much to adjust my work hours to Broward College. Overall, I couldn't afford to quit my full-time job at the hotel, but I just didn't know that I could ask Tom for more sessions. I didn't understand his offer for me back then. However, I told him that I was looking forward to working with him shortly.

When I was getting back for my first season to Broward, I reached out to Tom to tell him I was ready to work with goalkeepers. He didn't have to wait long to offer me my first job for him, and I took care of the goalkeepers from the beginning; at the same time, I was patiently getting ready to become a team coach — I just had to be more fluent in English. After the first season at Broward and Weston, I told Tom that I was ready to work with the teams as well. He knew that I was responsible with my work, so he wanted to help me with my coaching career. Tom put me into the coaching staff and was helping me out whenever I needed. With the first year at Broward, I was already coaching for over one year for Tom. I just didn't want to waste time between my duties at school and team practices. I met plenty of coaches in Weston, but Tom has become a very special one for me — he was my mentor who gave me advice on how to become a better coach in the USA.

Without knowing anyone in a foreign country, I could meet many people within my first year in Miami. Moreover, I could build a friendly relationship with those people who opened the door for my plan B in my life. I am still working with Tom, and I am thrilled to be a part of the Weston family. The risk of leaving Poland was huge, but I just had to be patient, and work hard to get some extra benefits in the new country. If I wouldn't be so determined to get a scholarship at the college level, I wouldn't meet coach Munga, and as a result, I couldn't meet Tom, so many of my plans wouldn't even work. I didn't know that I could receive that many benefits of playing soccer — I just couldn't believe it, but sometimes the hard work pays off in a different way than it was supposed to. As a result, I met significant people from the different side of the same environment — soccer.

LITTLE NOTE for coach Munga and Tom:

"I don't know if there are some words to thank you enough for helping me out. Coach Munga, thank you for seeing a potential in me as a responsible young man who deserved a shot to shine. Tom, I really appreciate that

you took care of me from the beginning, and I know that I can always count on your help. You guys opened me the door for my plan B — you gave me the chance to enter the gate as a coach, I just had to find the key to open it. THANK YOU!"

TWENTY-TWO

THE USA MODULE

One of the most important things to understand for a coach is the system where any trainer would like to be a part of. Even though I had some experience in Poland, the system of coaching is not the same everywhere in the world, especially in the U.S. Before I understood the methods of coaching in America, I had to play as a player at the college level; I had to read and listen to other coaches a lot, and most importantly, I had to study and start doing my coaching licenses from the U.S Soccer Center and United Soccer Coaches.

My first licenses were goalkeeping courses level 1 & 2. From the beginning, I just couldn't believe that young goalkeepers could become great athletes in that kind of system. Moreover, I didn't like the coaching points they were making, but I realized quickly that I wasn't there to modify the system, I was there to adjust and add my way of coaching. With that being said, I didn't argue with the instructor since I knew that he wouldn't give me the certification if I complained about their methods. With time, I understood that coaching in a different country equals to coaching in a unique system of the game. Moreover, the next licenses were supposed to prepare me to get an entire team, so I was getting my grassroots courses, and later, I wanted to make a D-license to improve my knowledge and opportunities from the coaching perspectives. One of the most important things I got from those courses was to never try to change the system. All I have to do to succeed as a coach in the USA is just to follow the rules which they told me about.

The American system was very complicated for me from the beginning, the soccer programs were just very different from the European ones. If I didn't get the experience as a college player, most likely, I would never understand the pyramid of success in the game. In Poland, the system is very simple to understand, but very tough for all athletes. You play at youth level where there are a couple of divisions, and the central league is the best in the country. However, later, athletes must move to the senior level, so either you are capable of playing pro or you aren't that good to join that level — it is that simple and sad at the same time. If you are 18 years old in Europe and you don't have a prospective contract with a pro team, most likely you will never make it to the next level — the brutal reality. However, the system in America is much different, especially after the youth level. Young athletes have the opportunity to go to college where many different levels are available; the major ones are NCAA, NAIA, and NJCAA. In that scenario, all athletes might experience something way bigger than just playing pro at some level in Europe. Most NCAA schools offer much better facilities than most of the teams at the highest level in Europe; moreover, athletes have the time to get their education and work on their weaknesses before they move to play pro. I would call it the second and last chance to make the farthest step in the career. I was proud to be a part of it, but most importantly, I have learned the system which millions of players would like to join. So, as a coach, I need to look from a fresh perspective on the whole system — the level might not be that high like back in Europe, but all athletes get more time to shine on the field.

Lastly, to succeed in the USA soccer path, athletes must present wonderful abilities outside the soccer field. The fundamental part of doing the sport is to get a degree during the way of a sports career. Everyone thinks they could play at the college level outside their countries; however, being an athlete in the United States is an honor to open the door to success in the future. There are millions of people who would like to come and join that system, so you must present outstanding abilities outside the field to be the special one; moreover, you must be able to pass the school. If you struggle in school in your country, that might be a problem for you since the USA module calls it STUDENT-ATHLETE. Don't try to change that, it won't work your way.

TWENTY-THREE

MENTORING BEGINS

My soccer journey wouldn't even start, and, most likely, it would end a long time ago without having great mentors by my side. There are plenty of tools to create or describe the best coaches, some of them are remarkable based on the tactical parts, some can improve your technical skills, but in my opinion, mentoring and leading people to success is the most important tool in the coaching dictionary.

As a player, I explained what mentor means to me. From the player's eyes, the mentor is somebody who has an enormous impact on your daily life. They can help you become a better human just because of their presence, and they might not even be aware of that. The mentor makes you work harder than ever. This individual cannot be easy for you, even if the mentor is your best friend, there is time to work and time to joke; the mentor knows how to manage it. If you think your world is falling apart, the mentor always says something that makes you believe in your dreams again. The mentor always is there for you to help, they care about your success. This person doesn't charge you for advice, the mentor is always for you when you need it.

As an athlete, I was looking for the best possible mentors, and I found plenty of them. I met some people who helped me with becoming a better soccer player, better coach, and better person in life. However, as soon as I became a coach, I knew that one of the most powerful things to do was to find the way to become a mentor for my young athletes. Firstly, I was following the advice from Jaro, the more experience I got — the better coach I could be. That's why I moved to the United States, where I joined the college team and completed my licenses. Knowing the European and American systems of the game were very powerful for me as for coach. Next, I know that playing as long as possible, especially at a good level, would bring the interest and trust from young candidates — the same scenario as I had with coach Krzyształowicz and coach Munga. Achieving something what young athletes dream about creates the perfect connection between me, coach, and my players. The more successful I am as a player, the bigger chance I have to be the mentor for everyone in that area. Lastly, the bigger knowledge I have both as a coach and as a player, the better advice I can give to my young players; for example, choosing the right team and later the college, finding the good agent to work with, etc. That's why education is extremely significant for me, and as a coach I don't see the different idea than graduating with my master's degree. In addition, all of this is required to work as a coach at the college level. I am sure that if I want to be a brilliant coach at any level, I must be a great mentor for everyone.

Finding a way to turn into a mentor for my young players has given me plenty of motivation to develop. I knew that every single minute I invested on the field as a player might not pay me back in my soccer career, but for sure, it would give me benefits back as for coach. That's why I believed that the more time I would invest, the more profits I would get in the close future. I wasn't scared of putting lots of effort in it because I understood that no matter how the soccer life went, I would be the winner either way. As a player, I dreamed of being the best on the field, but, as a coach, I wish to prepare my players to achieve their own dreams, and show them that everything is possible with the optimal attitude to work. Success can't always be described as a professional contract in the frame, but as a person you have become. By meeting all my mentors and learning from them, I would like to give this knowledge to others and help some people go further than I could. I hope that I will be able to make a difference in coaching as my coaches did in my life. At the same time, this is the hardest task to do as a coach. MAKING A DIFFERENCE = BEING A MENTOR.

TWENTY-FOUR

OTHER OPPORTUNITIES

P laying soccer gave me tons of benefits outside the field — I could meet great people, I could find mentors who gave me the advice for moving forward and defeating all my difficulties in my life. However, most importantly, soccer gave me the idea for my life. Before I came to the United States, I was honored to get experience at the highest level in Poland as a player while I was on the tryouts in Lech Poznań. Later, I got my first experience and possibility to become a coach. However, working with the best ones on a daily basis wasn't at my range when I was in Poland. My connections outside the field weren't that great as in the United States.

As soon as I came to the U.S, I met Munga, Broward College head coach. But most importantly, I met a coach who was really powerful in the soccer industry in the

United States. Everything I have done on the field for him brought me much more than I ever invested as a player — he gave me the opportunity to enter the adult's life. I always had plenty of ideas about what I would like to do, but in Poland my dreams were almost impossible to achieve. I have never had contact with bigger players than from Polish Ekstraklasa, but after coming to the U.S. I could join the Kicks International team, which gave me the opportunity to work with the best clubs — FC Barcelona, S.S.C. Napoli, and international teams, like Brazil, Colombia, and Peru. Moreover, I was offered to work regularly with Inter Miami CF. So, that time I was able to be around the most successful players and coaches around the world. To remind you, I've got all of those opportunities just because I did my job while I was playing soccer. The profits didn't show for me directly as a player, but it paid me off outside the field. That was the primary gate to my future direction.

In addition, investing my time as a coach helped me with meeting other great people around. Actually, all of them knew each other; for example, everyone knew Munga and everyone respected him a lot. Only because I have been doing my best as a coach, people around me, saw that I would be the one who deserved some chances for big offers. One day, I received a phone call from coach Vicky Ruiz, one of the coaches I have met in Weston, who recommended me for an influential position in Kentucky. I just got the contact information of the Louisville City FC head coach. The team is in the USL Championship, which is the second highest level in the U.S. They offered me to work there as a team administrator, and my duties would include taking care of the entire team and the logistic part. In the whole United States, there are probably only 40 spots for that job, and I've already got one. That's just crazy!

The hardest parts for me have been answering my question and being the prisoner of my own thoughts. All I wanted to do was to play soccer. Later, I have gotten plenty of offers, which were all great to take. And only I could make the decision which way I would like to go. Answering for the question — DO I REALLY WANT THIS? — makes it all much harder since I would love to have everything, but it's impossible. Everything comes down to the same thing, including taking a risk and finding the answer for that one the most troublesome question I could ask myself. Here we are again.

I am glad that I have that many opportunities, and no matter which way I would like to go, there are plenty of benefits of any choice. Just remember that I got those opportunities because I came back to the field even when I wasn't supposed to. I just couldn't leave soccer with no success, and the biggest victory for me is having all surrounding options.

TWENTY-FIVE

MY FUTURE GOALS

I remember that day when I wrote a postcard to myself — I wanted to make a contract with me, so I wouldn't quit until I got the things done. I haven't been on the tryouts in MLS as a player, but I worked for Inter Miami CF and was offered to work for Louisville City FC. In addition, I have accomplished the other task — I wrote my first book. Moreover, I understood that playing at the highest level would be possible for me if I could get one more chance to shine. However, even without achieving my one aim as a player, I have grown enough to set my future goals in my career. Setting the goals have become my routine, so here are some of them for the future:

- #1, Finally, I would like to find my peace with playing soccer as a player. I cannot wait to hear my remaining eligibility, and I hope that I will get at least one extra year to play for FGCU. However, if I don't get this chance, I am ready to move forward since I can say to myself — I DID MY BEST.
- #2, I am looking forward to getting my D-license, The Advanced National Goalkeeping Diploma which is the highest GK diploma in the USA at that moment, and I would like to get into an internship with an MLS team.
- #3, Getting my bachelor's and master's degrees from the USA.
- #4, Getting experience as a coach at the college, and soon, I would like to find the graduate position at D1 level.
- #5, Doing my best as a coach with my young players, being a mentor for them, and helping them to become better athletes.
- #6, My supreme goal is to become a head or GK coach and/or compliance officer for a university. I want to use my experience and help players like me to get their chance to play at the NCAA level.
- #7, Creating my own goalkeeper academy in the United States.

- #8, Being happy every day.

DO I REALLY WANT THIS?
YES.

Epilogue

On the way to success all details are important. I hope you are the one who will achieve greatness in sport. In 99.9% on the way to your dreams, you will have plenty of talks with yourself — DO I REALLY WANT THIS? The hardest part of this is that you are the only one who can answer that question. Don't let anyone break your character, don't let anyone ruin your dreams, and, most importantly, don't let yourself regret your final answer to our favorite question.

About the Author

My name is Michal Gorszczaryk, and this is my first book. I am the creator of MG keeper program. If you are interested in how my soccer journey continued — click on the link below.

If you have any questions or would like to collaborate — DM or email me.

Email: mgkeeper96@gmail.com

[O] instagram.com/mg_keeper

Made in the USA
Columbia, SC
25 April 2022

59459986R00138